IMAGES
of America

DUNBAR

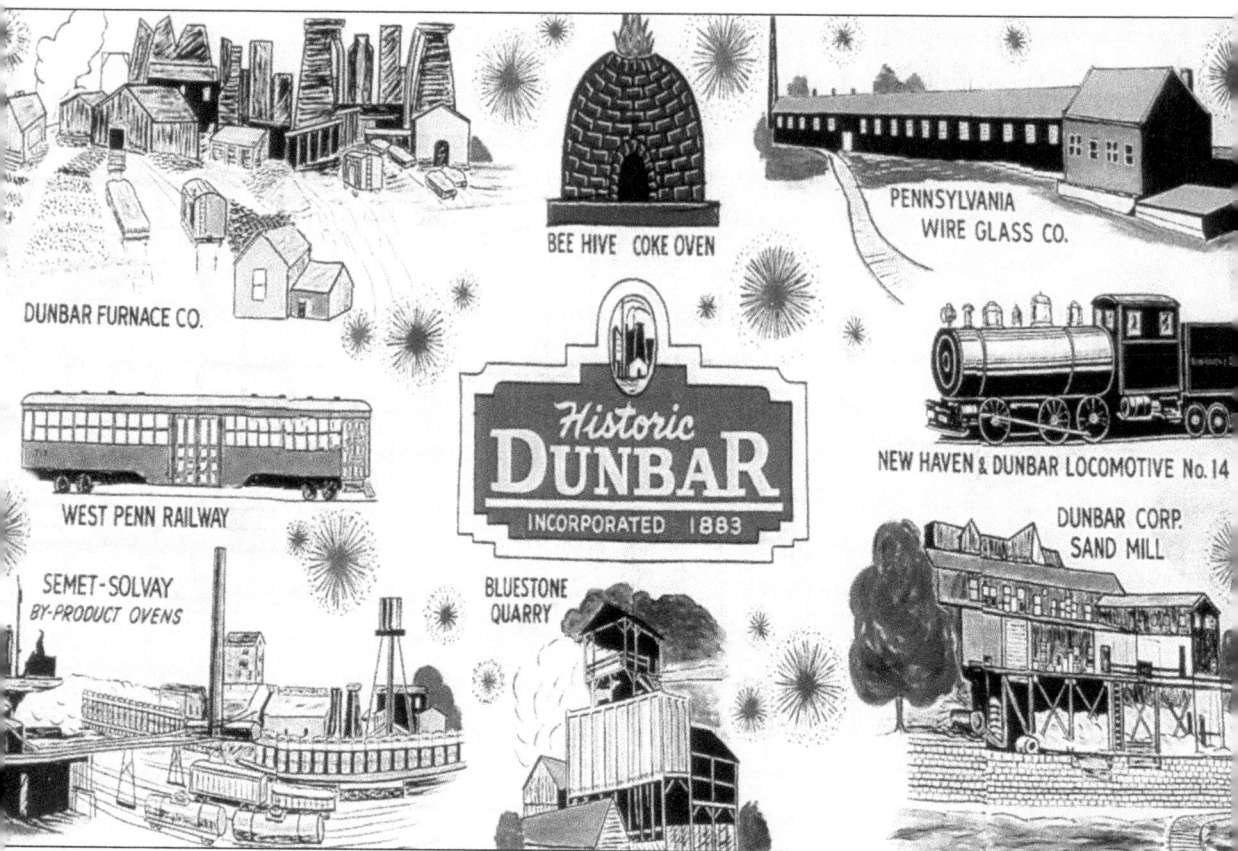

DUNBAR FURNACE CO.

BEE HIVE COKE OVEN

PENNSYLVANIA WIRE GLASS CO.

Historic DUNBAR INCORPORATED 1883

WEST PENN RAILWAY

NEW HAVEN & DUNBAR LOCOMOTIVE No. 14

SEMET-SOLVAY BY-PRODUCT OVENS

BLUESTONE QUARRY

DUNBAR CORP. SAND MILL

Hanging prominently on the former Central Bank building, this mural, commissioned by the Dunbar Historical Society in 2004 and painted by Connellsville artist Gerald Metzger, shows the many industries that helped to make Dunbar prosperous. (Courtesy of the Dunbar Historical Society Archives.)

On the cover: Built prior to 1901, George H. Swearingen's home on Church Street was located across from his general merchandise store, which was built in 1901. His first store burned down while he and his family were attending the 1893 World's Columbian Exposition. Born in 1853 in Hopwood, Swearingen was successful and highly respected, doing over $40,000 worth of business each year. He died in 1924. (Courtesy of the Clawson family.)

IMAGES
of America

DUNBAR

Dunbar Historical Society

ARCADIA
PUBLISHING

Copyright © 2009 by Dunbar Historical Society
ISBN 978-1-5316-4296-9

Published by Arcadia Publishing
Charleston SC, Chicago IL, Portsmouth NH, San Francisco CA

Library of Congress Control Number: 2009923684

For all general information contact Arcadia Publishing at:
Telephone 843-853-2070
Fax 843-853-0044
E-mail sales@arcadiapublishing.com
For customer service and orders:
Toll-Free 1-888-313-2665

Visit us on the Internet at www.arcadiapublishing.com

This book is dedicated to Col. Joan M. Graziano, whose dedication helped found the Dunbar Historical Society in 1995 and whose financial support helped purchase the education center in 2006.

CONTENTS

ACKNOWLEDGMENTS

The Dunbar Historical Society wishes to thank those who have contributed pictures for this work, including Arnold and Phyllis Brubaker, Curtis Lehman, Jerry and Christine Ryan, Dennis Morrison, Patrick Trimbath, Elizabeth A. Cross, Diana Homer, Carmella Hardy, George R. and Donna R. Myers, John and Bonnie Zurick Jr., Michael J. Bell, Patricia Paull Newsom, Warren Wortman, Albert Caruso, Krista D'Amico, Francis Sferro, Dave Moffett, Donna Murray, Patrick Maloy, Jon Marietta, Robert M. Martin, Gary Rockwell, Nick Bell Jr., Doris Lizza, Dearl Lowry, Angela Cooper, Lee Maley, Theresa Pockstaller, Joseph W. Martin, the Christopher Hughes family, the Collins family, the Rechenberg family, the Boy Scouts of America Troop 1-180 Archives, and the Clawson family. Thanks to everyone who has contributed photographs to the Dunbar Historical Society Archives.

Special thanks to Mary D. Ryan, whose photographs have provided a visual time capsule for the community; to all those with a camera in hand ready to photograph the everyday moments to capture Dunbar's history; and to citizens from the past who took the time to write about Dunbar. It is on their foundation of work that writers today have a basis for research.

Thanks to book committee members George R. and Donna R. Myers, Paul Trimbath, Patrick Trimbath, Elizabeth A. Cross, Dennis Morrison, William Suffern, John and Bonnie Zurick Jr., Louise Riggin, Carmella Hardy, Michael J. Bell, and Diana Homer.

Sincere gratitude is extended to editor Erin Vosgien, whose support, advice, and patience helped to guide the committee through the book-writing process.

The mission of the Dunbar Historical Society, a nonprofit 503(c) organization, is to collect and to preserve all material that will illustrate the history of Dunbar and to provide educational opportunities to ensure that present and future generations understand their rich heritage. Visit the society's Web site for information.

Unless otherwise credited, all images in this work appear courtesy of the Dunbar Historical Society Archives.

INTRODUCTION

Originally called Frogtown, either for the croaking critters or for the iron ones made at the furnace, Dunbar was settled in the 1790s and incorporated in 1883. The name was changed to Dunbar City and finally Dunbar. The town was named for Col. Thomas Dunbar, who was in charge of the 48th Regiment of Foot during the French and Indian War. Along with Gen. Edward Braddock, Dunbar came to America in 1755 to help regain Fort Duquesne. After the unbelievable defeat of Braddock's army at the Battle of the Monongahela, many believe Dunbar was a coward for leaving the area after Braddock's death. However, one must wonder with what troops, horses, and supplies Dunbar was to try to make a second stand. According to historian C. Hale Sipe,

> Dunbar has been greatly criticized on account of the slowness with which he followed Braddock, but it should be remembered that he had the poorest troops, many of whom sickened and died on the way. He had the heaviest stores and an insufficient number of horses to transport them and that he was almost constantly harassed by the French and Indians as his poor jaded horses dragged the heavily laden wagons up the mountain sides in the summer heat.

After the battle, fleeing wagoners and panicked troops took the horses. Many wagons were left with no horses to pull them, so they, along with the supplies, were destroyed at Dunbar's camp. Little is known of Dunbar after this incident. In 1755, he was sent into honorable retirement as lieutenant governor of Gibraltar and was never again actively employed in the military. He died in 1777. It is for this man that Dunbar was named.

Toward the end of the 1700s, the industrial age found its way to Dunbar. Isaac Meason, the area's first successful ironmaster, started his first Union Furnace in 1791 followed by his second Union Furnace at the same location in 1793. The building of Center Furnace and the first and second Laurel Furnace helped to make Dunbar an iron-making center in its early years. These furnaces marked the beginning of what would become Dunbar's lifeblood over the next century. Drawn to Dunbar by the prospect of work, the fabric of the community was made up of an ethnically rich and financially diverse population. As the iron was moved from the furnace to the creek near the former Bowest railroad yard, Connellsville Street became the main road through town. It was along this road that many of Dunbar's businesses sprang up, most to meet the needs of the changing community, its workers, and their families. Some of the early settlers in the area included Christopher Gist, Capt. George Paull, Col. James Paull, Isaac Meason, Thomas Watt, Andrew Bryson, John Speers, Samuel Pope, John Wortman, and Alexander Martin.

As part of the Connellsville coke region, which extended about 50 miles between Latrobe to the north and Fairchance to the south, Dunbar was vital to the development of steel in Pittsburgh. At the height of the coke era in 1899, all but 50 ovens in Fayette County were the beehive-type coke oven. These 50 ovens were the Semet-Solvay Company by-product ovens. These by-product ovens were the first ones built in the United States outside the home plant in New York. The Semet-Solvay ovens captured and reused the by-products of the coke-burning process, making Dunbar one of the first towns in the United States to recycle. Between the time of Meason's first iron furnace through the 1960s, Dunbar was home to the Union Furnace, which became the Dunbar Furnace; Semet-Solvay by-product ovens; Pennsylvania Wire Glass Company; the bluestone quarry; a sand plant; several brickworks; an ice plant; a woolen mill; the Bowest rail yards (so named because both the Baltimore and Ohio and the Western Maryland Railroads used them); a fireworks plant; several sawmills; a gristmill; and mines and coke oven sites with names like Hill Farm, Ferguson, Atlas, Mahoning, Watt, Anchor, and Uniondale, the vestiges of which still stand as "beehive sentinels" around the community today.

Beautiful homes and buildings, like the Hotel Central and the George H. Swearingen General Merchandise Store and home were built between 1890 and 1920. While many homes were sparse and simply furnished, others were large multistory buildings with beautiful facades and balconies. Many of these historic homes and buildings remain standing today as a testament to a more prosperous time.

Not untouched by tragedy, Dunbar has weathered extraordinary disasters, including major floods in 1895, 1907, 1912, 1954, and 1972; devastating block-long fires; and the devastating June 16, 1890, Hill Farm Mine explosion. Prior to the Hill Farm Mine disaster, the Uniondale Mine, owned by the Reid brothers, had two fatal explosions. The first, on November 28, 1878, killed 6 and seriously injured 10 others, and the second, on March 8, 1886, killed 4 miners and a trackman. Two explosions at the Keystone Fireworks plant resulted in loss of life. In 1948, Pauline Nativio was killed, and in 1966, Louise Ross, Helen Tonio, Freda Bezilla, Jo McNatt, and Anna Mae Widener were killed. Dunbar has survived the ravages of nature, the ever-changing industrial climate, the sadness of loss as a result of local disasters, and the erosion and loss of its financial base. No matter what disaster befell the town, the hearty people who called Dunbar home rallied to overcome adversity time and time again.

The first train service to reach Dunbar was the Baltimore and Ohio Railroad in 1859. The Pennsylvania track was completed in 1876. Initially, the Baltimore and Ohio Railroad had a small flag station near the mill. A larger station was built in the downtown area in 1866, followed in later years by a third station at the same location. The Pennsylvania Railroad station was built in 1876. Both stations handled large amounts of train traffic. With the decline of train traffic, both stations were torn down in the 1950s and 1960s. Trolley service through town began in 1903 when the Pittsburgh, McKeesport and Connellsville Railway extended its line to the Dunbar area and by 1905 merged with a second company to form the West Penn Railways Company. The trolley opened up a new era of travel for residents that peaked in ridership around 1924. After that time, an increase in the use of automobiles, a declining population, and the advent of the Depression started the decline of the trolley, which ceased operations on August 9, 1952. The death of the trolley was memorialized by the Dunbar citizenry when a group chartered a special streetcar dubbed the "Dunbar Special" in order to bury the last trolley. The local undertaker, J. T. Burhans, provided the small coffin, and other riders acted as pallbearers, going as far as wearing swallowtail coats for the funeral. The trolley was draped with banners proclaiming, "So Long West Penn Trolley" and "Dunbar's Last Car Ride." When the Dunbar revelers arrived in Connellsville and Uniontown, they got off the trolley carrying the small coffin and paraded around the terminals complete with mourners and requiem music. Dunbar folk knew how to send off an old friend, and this event went down as one of the most memorable of Dunbar celebrations.

Dunbar has always been home to dedicated folks who have struggled to improve their community. Many are the descendants of the first settlers in the area and when asked about

Dunbar speak with pride that few towns can claim. Much of Dunbar's oral history has been handed down from generation to generation. Dunbar can also claim some colorful characters who helped make life in Dunbar unique. One of those characters was O'Neal Medore. Born in 1900, he worked at the Dunbar Furnace and the Pennsylvania Wire Glass Company. He achieved success in the field of aeronautics and taught local flying classes. He was a licensed pilot and was one of Dunbar's first residents to own his own plane. Town folks remember him best for building an airplane in his garage only to find he could not get it out of the building when completed. He drove his old steam shovel around his property blowing the horn in order to thwart what he perceived as FBI surveillance. He died in 1991 at the ripe old age of 91.

Evidence of the faith of this small community is readily apparent. Dunbar's religious roots run deep, and many of the early church congregations remain active in town to this day. Running equally as deep is the patriotism of the residents. The Dunbar Honor Roll, built in 1944 as a memorial to those men and women who proudly served in every war since the Revolutionary War, is a testament to the pride the community holds for its military history. Formed in 1942, the Victory Park Association supervised the design and construction of the honor roll. Many designs were submitted, with the design of Philadelphia's J. Roy Carroll Jr. being chosen. He contributed the design free of charge. About 75 percent of the work on the memorial was completed using donated labor. The honor roll was built from the remains of the Fairview School and fieldstones and cut stones from the Harper's woolen mill. The impressive structure, located in Memorial Park, overlooks the small town.

Education was a priority for local children. Prior to consolidation, each area of Dunbar and its environs had a local school with names like Fayette, Dunbar Borough, Fairview, Pechin, Gettemy, Furnace, Liston, Hughes, Hennessey, Harper's, Hill Farm, and St. Aloysius Catholic School. The one-room log Franklin School, one of the earliest in the area, was built in 1832 and burned down in 1840. Public schooling began in Dunbar in early 1835, and the first report by law was made in October 1835. Like most towns, Dunbar had many organizations that met at various locations in town. These organizations provided fraternal, social, and educational opportunities for young and old alike. Some of them were the Knights of the Golden Eagle, the Knights of Pythias, the Ladies Aid Society, the Independent Order of Odd Fellows, the Lions Club, the Irishtown and Dunbar Sportsmen Clubs, the American Legion, and Boy and Girl Scout troops.

Never to be questioned is the community pride that has been passed down from one generation to the next. The 1915 old home week event was the watershed of celebrations. The entire town plus hundreds of visitors were in attendance for the parades, games, and speeches that took place during the three-day event. Fantastic decorations were in evidence on the buildings, homes, cars, buggies, and even the people. Today the annual Dunbar Community Fest, held the last Saturday of September, draws hundreds of people to town. In 2008, Dunbar celebrated its 125th anniversary of incorporation with the dedication of a clock in the downtown area.

Another constant over the years has been the many pastimes in which children and adults have participated. Families were large, and with money tight, most activities took place in town. Sports, especially football and baseball, took center stage and provided hours of enjoyment and competition for area youth. Dunbar can lay claim to many championships throughout the years. Not lacking in the artistic area, Dunbar's local artists have created stone sculptures and paintings that remain today as reminders that Dunbar's heritage is more than just industrial. No discussion of Dunbar would be complete without noting the rich hunting and fishing history in the area. Originally the source of food for many mountain and valley families, today Dunbar Creek and the Dunbar Mountains offer sporting opportunities not found in other areas. Dunbar has a long and varied musical history. Catherine Williams, a local piano teacher, came from England and called Dunbar her home until her death in 1969. Prior to her death, almost all area children took lessons from her. Dunbar music went beyond formal piano lessons. Any discussion of music in town would not be complete without acknowledging the importance of its mountain music, which is renowned for its fiddlers, fifers, singers, and musical families. One of the most famous fiddlers was David Gilpin, who lost his ring finger and the use of his little finger in an accident. Not to be deterred from his fiddling passion, he relearned how to play his fiddle with only two fingers. Names like Jim Bryner, Denune "Nooney" Provance, John Wesley Devan, and Sam Waggle helped to establish Dunbar's rich musical heritage. As a result of the efforts of these people and many others to keep this music alive, the Old Time Fiddler's Association was formed and still meets monthly at the Fayette County Fairgrounds.

While the industry is gone and the population has decreased, Dunbar continues to exist along the banks of the beautiful Dunbar Creek as a testament to the proud residents who still call it home. This book chronicles roughly 150 years of Dunbar history, from the first furnace through the boom days to the gradual downturn and loss of its industrial base to some unique tourism opportunities that are helping to bring the little town back to life. In 2006, the Fayette Central Railroad tourist train began operating between Uniontown and Dunbar; the Sheepskin Trail, the first spur off the Great Allegheny Passage, opened in 2008; and the Dunbar Historical Society's rebuilding of a coke oven at its park promises to revive the little town. Along with these exciting tourism opportunities, the history of the town will continue to be collected, compiled, and shared with present and future generations through educational programming by the members and friends of the Dunbar Historical Society.

One

BUSINESS AND INDUSTRY

Donated to the Dunbar Historical Society by artist William (Bill) Rockwell, this drawing shows the 1854 Dunbar Furnace. Built by Isaac Meason, the Union Furnace name was changed in 1844 to Dunbar Furnace under the management of Jones and Miller. In 1854, Baldwin and Cheney discontinued the use of charcoal as fuel and began using coke. One of Dunbar's leading citizens, Thomas W. Watt, was general superintendent for Baldwin and Cheney.

These four panoramic views from about 1915 show the industry in the valley between Hardy Hill and Furnace Hill just outside Dunbar Borough. From top to bottom are the Pennsylvania Wire Glass Company and three views of the Semet-Solvay Company and the Dunbar Furnace Company. (Courtesy of George R. and Donna R. Myers.)

In 1895, the first contract to build a block of Semet-Solvay by-product coke ovens, outside the home plant in New York, was made with the Dunbar Furnace Company. The 50 ovens were to supply the furnaces with coke, and the by-products—coal tar, ammonia, gas, and light oil—were used for other industries. The gas was used by the Pennsylvania Wire Glass Company.

In 1791, Isaac Meason started a small furnace on Dunbar Creek, and in 1793, Meason and Dillon built a larger furnace and foundry at the same site. In 1844, Jones and Miller changed the name from Union to Dunbar Furnace and used water from Dunbar Creek as the motive power. In 1852, Watt and Larmer installed the first steam boiler and hot blast stove at the furnace. Baldwin and Cheney were the first to use coke as fuel in 1854. The Youghiogheny Coal and Iron Company assumed operations at the furnace in 1860 and moved it about 300 yards downstream. The Dunbar Iron Company, with Edmund Pechin as superintendent, became the owner in 1866. The furnace was compelled to close down in 1873, and in 1874, the Dunbar Iron Company sold out. In 1876, the Dunbar Furnace Company was formed. It took over the holdings of the Dunbar Iron Company. Pechin remained superintendent. By 1880, the company purchased the Ferguson ovens and built 98 beehive ovens at Hill Farm Mine.

This photograph shows a rare glimpse into the inside of the Dunbar Furnace Company. The furnace workers included many boys who were put to work at a young age to help supplement the family income. Changes in the physical structure of the plant are evident where the wall was simply torn out to make way for modernization and changes in the plant.

Dunbar Furnace Company employees are, from left to right, James McVey, George Gilroy, John McVey, James Martin, Joseph O'Neal, George Frye, Michael Flynn, Archie Reid, Jacob Breakiron, and Doc Smitley. Work at the furnace was dirty, and employees put in many hours since labor laws had not yet been passed. Many of the furnace pictures were donated to the Dunbar Historical Society by the Lawrence Harvey estate.

The photograph above shows the internal workings of the Dunbar Furnace Company. It appears that repairs are being made to the equipment. The date of the photograph and the men are unidentified. Hundreds of workers came from far and wide to work at the furnace, which was the largest employer at one time. As many immigrants flocked to the mines, most who came to work had little money. The company paid the miner with scrip redeemable only at the company store. The scrip (below) was issued by the Dunbar Furnace Company store. While providing for the workers and their families, the use of scrip and company housing was also a way of keeping the men from leaving the employ of the company. (Courtesy of George R. and Donna R. Myers.)

DUNBAR FURNACE STORE.

GOOD FOR _____

in merchandise at my Store.

J. M. HUSTEAD.

$1.

Per _____

5	40	75	110	145	180	215	250	285	320	355	390	425	460	495
10	45	80	115	150	185	220	255	290	325	360	395	430	465	**500**
15	50	85	120	155	190	225	260	295	330	365	**400**	435	470	
20	55	90	125	160	195	230	265	**300**	335	370	405	440	475	
25	60	95	130	165	**200**	235	270	305	340	375	410	445	480	
30	65	**100**	135	170	205	240	275	310	345	380	415	450	485	
35	70	105	140	175	210	245	280	315	350	385	420	455	490	

Cleaning mined coal was practiced little in Fayette County due to the purity of the coal from the Pittsburgh bed. According to the June 12, 1905, issue of *Fuel* magazine, the Link-Belt Machinery Company of Chicago installed the first coal washer in Dunbar at the Semet-Solvay Company for its by-product ovens. Coal from the Freeport mines was treated at the washer, which operated until 1924. (Courtesy of George R. and Donna R. Myers.)

One of Dunbar's largest employers was the Pennsylvania Wire Glass Company. The Continuous Glass Press Company began in April 1904. The name was changed to the Pennsylvania Wire Glass Company in 1910. The company was purchased for $125,000 by a group of stockholders in 1943. G and W Wire Glass of New Castle bought it in 1961 and auctioned the plant, equipment, and land in 1963.

In 1869, Bliss and Marshall began manufacture of firebrick at the brickworks at Pechin. George C. Marshall Sr., of Bliss and Marshall, was the father of Gen. George C. Marshall, who authored the Marshall Plan after World War II and who became secretary of state in 1947. Works in town were operated by the Dunbar Fire Brick Company in 1890 and United Fire Brick Company in 1907. A brickworks in the Susan Street and Fayette Street area made bricks with the word *Dunbar* impressed into them. The decline of the brick industry closely followed the decline of the coke industry.

American Manganese Company employees pose for the camera around 1920. The American Manganese Company of Philadelphia was formed in 1914 when the Dunbar Furnace Company was forced to reorganize. In 1924, the American Manganese Company was forced by a Philadelphia court order to be offered at public sale. This action sounded the death knell for the iron industry in the Dunbar area.

The earliest evidence of sand making in the Dunbar area was in 1869 when a news article noted the Dunbar Iron Company sand mill had a capacity of 25 to 30 tons a day. Dunbar's white silica sand was known far and wide for its purity. In 1915, the largest plant in the country on Irishtown Run produced 500 to 600 tons of sand daily. The plant changed hands several times. James Bryner was one of the first laborers and later the superintendent of the mill. He began work in 1925 at the highest quarry on the hill and was there when the plant ceased operations in September 1954. He wrote "Ode to Dunbar Sand," expressing sorrow at the loss of Dunbar's sand industry.

Quarrying of Loyalhanna limestone, called bluestone because of its color, may have started as early as 1803. The earliest lease by Sarah Harper to Albert Scott occurred in 1887. The Dunbar Creek valley had exposed bluestone on both sides of the mountain. Sand, sandstone blocks, iron ore, firestone, fireclay, and coal were quarried. The tipple (right) is where crushed stone was loaded onto railcars using a spur built by the Dunbar Furnace Company. Bluestone blocks, known as Belgian blocks, were used in building, construction, and paving. They were hand cut by 150 stonecutters and 150 laborers. Years after the tipple was dismantled, the resourcefulness of Dunbar native Oliver Wayne Martin turned the remaining tipple base on the creek side into Rippling Waters Restaurant (below). It closed in the late 1960s or early 1970s.

In March 1935, the Interstate Amiesite Corporation started making road-paving material. It was located diagonally across from the Harper's School. The plant closed in 1978 after being in business for 43 years. Prior to being torn down, the plant buildings stood for many years. Henry Bunting was the office clerk in 1935 and plant manager in 1945. The first employees hired were Ross May, Dewey Eans, and William James.

The Dunbar Ice Company, incorporated in March 1907, operated until about 1920. Starting with capital of $15,000, the owners were George McCormick, Upton Speer, Charles McGee, Peter Johnson, and Milton Williams. The plant sold artificial ice. In the 1870s, Dunbar's natural ice was advertised for sale as "sweet-mountain water." In the late 1800s, George H. Swearingen sold blocks of ice from Lucas Pond at his store located on Connellsville Street.

Eureka Fire Brick was located about three miles southwest of Dunbar. The company started operations about 1883. Prior to that time, the works were managed by the Mount Braddock Fire Brick Company. At peak production, 12,000 coke oven, building, or paving bricks could be made each day. The largest trade was in coke oven brick, with the primary market being the southwestern Pennsylvania coke regions.

This vintage picture shows the Eureka Fire Brick workers. The small banner at the top appears to show the date of 1918, and there are Buy More Bonds signs on the wall behind the group. The man in the center is holding an award indicating that some goal was achieved, possibly related to the sale of war bonds.

The Strickler-Lowry mill (above), built in 1815, was commonly referred to as Speers Mill. It used the fast-flowing waters of Dunbar Creek to power its grindstones. In early years, a sawmill and distillery were part of the works. Converted to a roller mill in the late 1800s, it was located in the present-day vacant lot south of the block housing the Burhans-Crouse Funeral Home. Seen below, the builder's name stone, "Strickler & Lowry A.D. 1815," was located at the gable end of the structure and is now owned by John Mancini, who permitted the photograph to be taken for this work. (Above, courtesy of the Clawson family; below, courtesy of John and Bonnie Zurick Jr.)

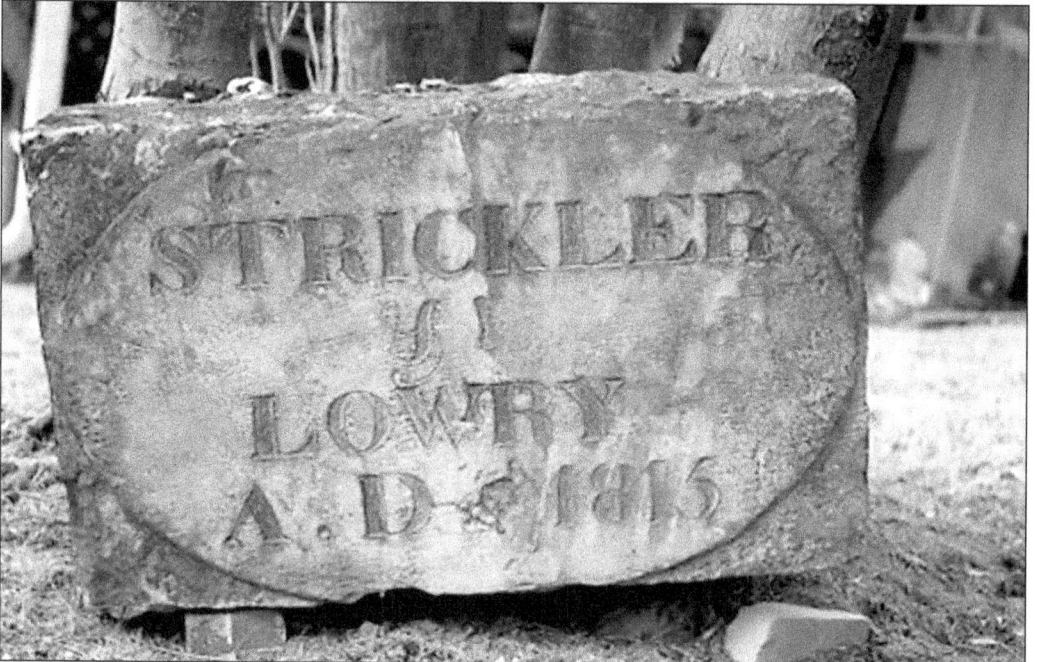

One of Dunbar's most beautiful buildings was the George H. Swearingen General Merchandise Store (above), constructed in 1901. Swearingen (right) was born in 1853 and in 1876 became a partner with George W. Porter in the mercantile business. He bought Porter out in 1880. He married Sarah Porter and had two daughters, Mae and Sadie, who died as a child. Appointed Dunbar postmaster by Pres. William McKinley in 1897, Swearingen owned a lot of property in town, was a member of the Royal Arcanum, was a 32nd-degree Mason, was a member of the Presbyterian Church, and was an active member of the Republican Party. His family name was originally Van Swearingen, and after his ancestors arrived in America in 1664 from Holland, some family lines dropped the Van from their names. Swearingen died in 1924 and is buried at Oak Grove Cemetery in Uniontown.

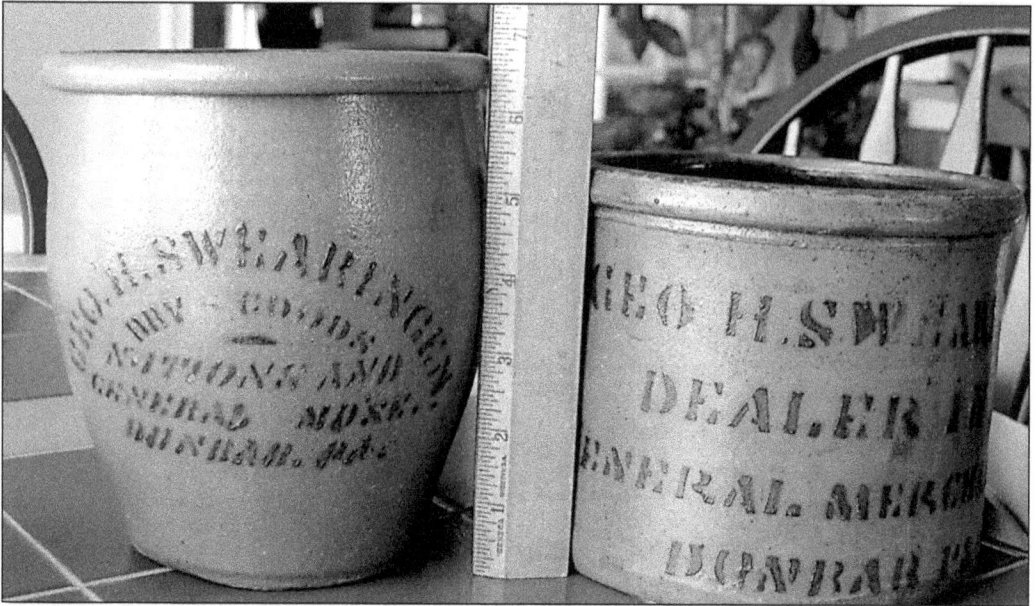

Some of the most valued advertising items today are the crocks that stores used in the course of everyday business. One provider of these crocks was the George H. Swearingen General Merchandise Store located on Railroad Street. Made by either the New Geneva Stoneware Company or Hamilton and Jones Stoneware Company, the crock (left) advertises "dry goods, notions and general md'se." (Courtesy of George R. and Donna R. Myers.)

With so many stores in Dunbar at the height of the economic boom, advertising became an important part of business. The Dunbar Supply Company sold "Wm. J. Moxley's Special Oleomargarine," which came from the company with the advertising stenciled on the crock, with only the store name being changed. (Courtesy of John and Bonnie Zurick Jr.)

Over the years, three locations in Dunbar were referred to as the Dunbar House. The first, a three-story frame building on Railroad Street, burned down in 1893. The second, also known as the Mahaney Hotel and located in the present-day Dunbar Historical Society park, burned down in 1896. The third (above) was the most famous and most recognizable. It was located on Connellsville Street and was built in 1897. It burned down on December 30, 1917. Fires plagued Dunbar throughout its early history. The fire that burned this Dunbar House jumped the street and burned the front of a building owned by George H. Swearingen, which was located next door to his home. His newest building, built in 1901, was not damaged in this fire. With the chartering of the Dunbar Volunteer Fire Company in 1923, block-long fires became a thing of the past. (Courtesy of George R. and Donna R. Myers.)

The Hotel Central (above) was built by David Christopher Foltz (left) in 1898 at a cost of $30,000. It was considered one of the finest and best-equipped hotels not only in Fayette County but also in the United States. Returning to Dunbar in 1883, Foltz began a successful career as an undertaker and became one of Fayette County's first embalmers, conducting more than 4,000 funerals during his lifetime. In addition to doing contracting work, he was engaged in building furniture. Locally, he owned 18 rental homes. He was married to Mary Cameron, and they had 12 children. He was one of the largest property owners and highest taxpayers in Dunbar and served on the council and the school board. He was a member of the Methodist Protestant Church. The portrait of Foltz was found in *Nelson's Biographical Dictionary and Historical Reference Book of Fayette County, Pennsylvania.* (Courtesy of George R. and Donna R. Myers.)

The First National Bank was built over Dunbar Creek in 1906. While undertaker J. N. Burhans was having the building constructed, the Dunbar Bank Limited purchased it. The Dunbar Bank Limited moved three times prior to the name being changed to the First National Bank and opening in the building over the creek.

Just before 1900, David Williams built this store on Railroad Street. Prior to that, he operated a store near the Strickler-Lowry gristmill. He operated the Railroad Street store until his death in 1922. His sons Milton and Harry took over the business until their deaths in 1949 and 1957, respectively. Williams's brother John was killed in the Reid brothers' Uniondale Mine explosion on March 8, 1886.

Dunbar Bakery was owned by the Wishart family and located on Railroad Street. Advertisements from vintage newspapers indicate the bakery was open as early as 1913 but possibly before. Family members shown are, from left to right, Andrew (father), Catharine, Florence, and Andrew Jr. sitting on mother Florence's lap. Catharine married Paul Rechenberg in 1935 and, after some remodeling, lived in the house for 67 years. The house still stands. (Courtesy of the Rechenberg family.)

Located in the Central Bank building and dressed up for the 1915 old home week celebration is the William S. Gaddis store. Gaddis (presumed to be on the right) was born in 1853 and educated at Waynesburg College before working at several different clerk jobs at various Dunbar businesses. He started his general merchandise store in 1886 and married Annie Hennon in 1888. They had eight children.

Shown in 1941, H. P. Smith Meat Market was operated by Cecil and Harold Smith. Located across from the Baltimore and Ohio Railroad station, the storefront was a mere sidewalk's width away from the railroad tracks. Meat, butchered on-site, along with a well-stocked supply of groceries, kept this market in business for many years. The business was purchased by the Kimmel family. The building burned down around 1970. The people pictured are unidentified.

The McGee Store, first located on Railroad Street, moved to the First National Bank building in May 1906. Richard McGee moved to Dunbar in 1886 and was appointed postmaster by Pres. Woodrow Wilson in July 1913. He moved to Uniontown in 1925 and worked at the courthouse until he was 90 years old. He died in 1954. His son merchant R. C. McGee had a cash store on Railroad Street in the Lang building.

Through the years, Dunbar celebrations were well known for their fireworks displays put on by the local fireworks company that is still in operation. The plant was established around 1912 and incorporated in 1916 as the American-Italian Fireworks Company. In the 1920s, it was reorganized as the Continental Fireworks Company, owned by the Lizza and DeBlasio families. Reorganization occurred again in 1948, when the company was named Keystone Fireworks and Specialty Company. It was owned by Bedy Lizza and Ernest DeBlasio. Today Keystone Fireworks is owned by Dawson resident Buck Newill. DeBlasio is seen above making a display. Holding a large firework below is Harry Lizza, along with, from left to right, Willie Lizza, DeBlasio, and an unidentified man.

Dunbar was home to many small grocery stores throughout the years, but their locations have been forgotten. Evident in this photograph of the Peoples Store (above) is its going-out-of-business promotion, "the most terrific slaughter of high class merchandise ever attempted." The window of the Walton store (below) is typical of the advertising and products the stores sold. All people are unidentified. Other grocery stores that called Dunbar home were the Soldano and Visconti Bank and Grocery, Frank Bell Store, Guy DiNello Grocery, DeMarco Store, Rose Izzo Grocery, Annie Rose Grocery, Rankin and Mitchell Grocery, McGee Store, David Williams Store, Smith-Muscenti Grocery, Samuel Davidson Butter Store, H. P. Smith Meat Market, and Nick Bell Store. Other names have been lost to history.

Roy and Freda Collins operated Collins Restaurant, located in the Burhans building, in the early 1960s. Through the years, this location housed the Reed Family Ice Cream Parlor, Don Fosselman Dairy Bar, Italio Tristani Dairy Bar, Marie Hagner Dairy Bar, and Jim Stefano's television and sporting goods store. The location is now part of the Burhans-Crouse Funeral Home. (Courtesy of the Collins family.)

Albert "Cutty" Caruso from Dunbar (second from left) is seen building a series of block ovens in the 1950s near Homer City. On the left are the beehive ovens that are completed but not yet covered, while on the right is the second row of ovens in various stages of completion. The oven being rebuilt by the Dunbar Historical Society will be a single beehive, as seen here. Others in the photograph are unidentified. (Courtesy of Albert Caruso.)

Cambria Iron Company started in Johnstown in 1852, and between 1889 and the early 1900s, it owned the Anchor, Mahoning, and Atlas Mines in Dunbar. The latter two mines were combined underground in 1902. This vintage photograph is titled "Cambria Iron Company's Coke Works, Morrell." Shown are mine workers, coke ovens, tipples, and lorry cars at the works around 1880. The lorry cars can be seen in the background transporting coal to the ovens from the tipples. The Dunbar Township area called Sitka became known as Morrell. It was named for Daniel Johnson Morrell (1821–1885), the general manager of the Cambria Iron Company, pictured at right. During the 1860s, he was a member of the U.S. House of Representatives. The USS *Morrell* was named after him. (Above, courtesy of Theresa Pockstaller.)

The Mahoning Mine and ovens were owned by several companies beginning in 1872, including Paull, Brown and Company; Mahoning Coke Company; Cambria Iron Company; and Cambria Steel Company. In 1875, the works had 100 beehive ovens, and by 1905, it had 136 ovens. It was through this mine that rescuers tried to reach the workers trapped in the Hill Farm Mine explosion in 1890. Due to incorrect maps, rescue efforts were futile.

The remains of the Mahoning Mine ovens still exist off Ranch Road in Dunbar. These were block ovens that were built in two long rows back to back. This photograph shows an oven in disrepair, but the top of the beehive oven can be seen above the front opening. The beehive top would not be visible if the oven was in working condition.

As a result of the Great Depression and the decline of Dunbar's industrial base, many men and families found themselves out of work with no prospect of employment. During that time, the ovens that were formerly the basis behind the area's economy took on a new role as homes for those displaced by the economic downturn. Here an unidentified man willingly poses for this photograph.

Coke oven homes filled the needs of people who had nowhere else to live. A crude table can be seen inside the oven. As late as the 1950s, it was not uncommon for oven dwellers in need of staples like coffee and sugar to knock on the doors of Dunbar residents, requesting a helping hand.

By 1880, the Dunbar Furnace Company owned the Ferguson works. Before 1880, Hogsett and Beal and then the Frick Company owned it. In 1875, there were 70 beehive ovens at the works. A freak explosion occurred at the mine in 1903, killing 18 workers. The Ferguson Mine and Hill Farm Mine, where an 1890 explosion occurred, were combined in 1905. The last-known owner was the United Refractories Company around 1920.

This trade card says it all: "The Boss Store for Everything & Everybody." With ties to several prominent Americans like Patrick Henry, James Madison Reid was born in West Newton on April 10, 1849. He came to Dunbar and engaged in the mercantile business for six years, beginning around 1868. According to John M. Gresham and Samuel T. Wiley, he was a man of great determination, fine intelligence, and business energy. (Courtesy of George R. and Donna R. Myers.)

Two

Town Scenes

This old town view shows Dunbar Borough between 1874 and 1901, as seen from the Speers Hill area of town. The business district is located at the center right with the long building being the Baltimore and Ohio Railroad station. Looking closer, several churches can be seen as well as many of the town's historic buildings.

Two Connellsville Street scenes show the main road through town where many of the early businesses sprang up. The photograph above shows the George H. Swearingen building (back left) and the Central Bank building (center). The bank was built in 1901 by Charles B. Nemon and operated until the 1930s. The building was constructed to the exact footprint of the property, which accounts for its peculiar shape. Its architecture makes it one of the most unique in town. Today the building is home to the Dunbar Borough Council chambers, a dentist office, and apartments. The photograph below shows the opposite Connellsville Street view with the Dunbar House (left) and Methodist Episcopal church (right). The trolley has already arrived in town, but the horse and buggy were still in use. (Courtesy of George R. and Donna R. Myers.)

This uniquely shaped Dunbar landmark was the Central Drugstore. While no building date is known, the Nemon family owned it beginning in 1904. The building's triangular design had 18-inch walls with a foundation inside a concrete wall to turn back the waters of Dunbar Creek. Seven-foot-thick stone footers could be seen in the basement when the building was torn down.

In an early Dunbar scene, the burgess office is shown at the left. The window also advertises oysters for 25¢ each. At left center is the H. P. Smith Meat Market building, and across the track is the Baltimore and Ohio Railroad station. The Central Drugstore is partially seen on the right along with an overturned wagon in the foreground. (Courtesy of George R. and Donna R. Myers.)

This property was originally the location of Kelly's Jewelry Store, which was washed away in the 1912 flood. The Sons of Italy building was constructed after that date. By 1922, Edwin and Charles Harvey operated a pool hall in the building. Harvey's Pool Hall was famous for its boiled hot dog sandwiches. Between 1947 and 1951, Frank Rose had a pool hall and bowling alley there. The Sons of Italy Lodge purchased the building from Rose in 1951. Originally called the Societa Italians Di Muto Succorse when the Italians organized in 1908, the group was granted a charter in 1909 and functioned until 1917 before incorporating with the Sons of Italy in 1918. Today the building is the home of the Kountry Klub Restaurant. The man pictured is unidentified.

This photograph shows the Jasper Martin farm at Irishtown near Dunbar. Martin was the grandfather of Robert M. Martin, whose family has deep roots in the Irishtown area. Clearing trees and brush are, from left to right, Pattie McCormick, William Martin, Abe Brooks, Charles Newton Martin, and Dennis Irvin Martin, Robert M. Martin's father. (Courtesy of Robert M. Martin.)

Known as the Dunbar Reservoir, the original name of the reservoir was the Porter Hill Reservoir. It was built between 1898 and 1904. Located above Dunbar in the High Street area of town, the reservoir was surrounded by wrought-iron fencing. This fencing was donated to the Dunbar Historical Society for its coke oven park project by the North Fayette County Municipal Authority.

This beautiful home was located on Railroad Street in Dunbar. Residents never missed the chance to have their picture taken. Family photographs were cherished items that passed down from one generation to the next. These are the images that provide the glimpses into Dunbar's past. At one time, this house was used by Dr. Harold Newill and family. The people pictured here are unidentified. (Courtesy of Warren Wortman.)

The Wilhelm home was located at the bottom of "Lock-Up Hill," so named because a jail was once located on the hill leading out of Dunbar. The Wilhelm property was home to Wilhelm Grocery and Wilhelm Photography. Home owners took pride in their homes and had beautiful flowers. Vegetable gardens, grown to meet the needs of large families, were also a common sight. The man pictured is unidentified.

Spanning the valley between Church Hill and Pechin Hill, this trestle was used by the railroad that serviced the mines outside town. Due to the loss of the mining industry that it served, the trestle was taken down in 1976 when it was no longer needed. St. Aloysius Catholic church, school, and convent can be seen in the background.

First National Bank Building Being Built (Was Built Over Dunbar Creek–No Longer Standing) Photo from Redding Bunting Collection

This photograph shows the building of the First National Bank over Dunbar Creek in 1906. The three-story building occupied the entire span of the creek. Home to many businesses through the years, it was torn down to make room for the new Connellsville Street bridge. In the 1850s, this was a covered bridge, according to a speech delivered at the old home week celebration by James Cray.

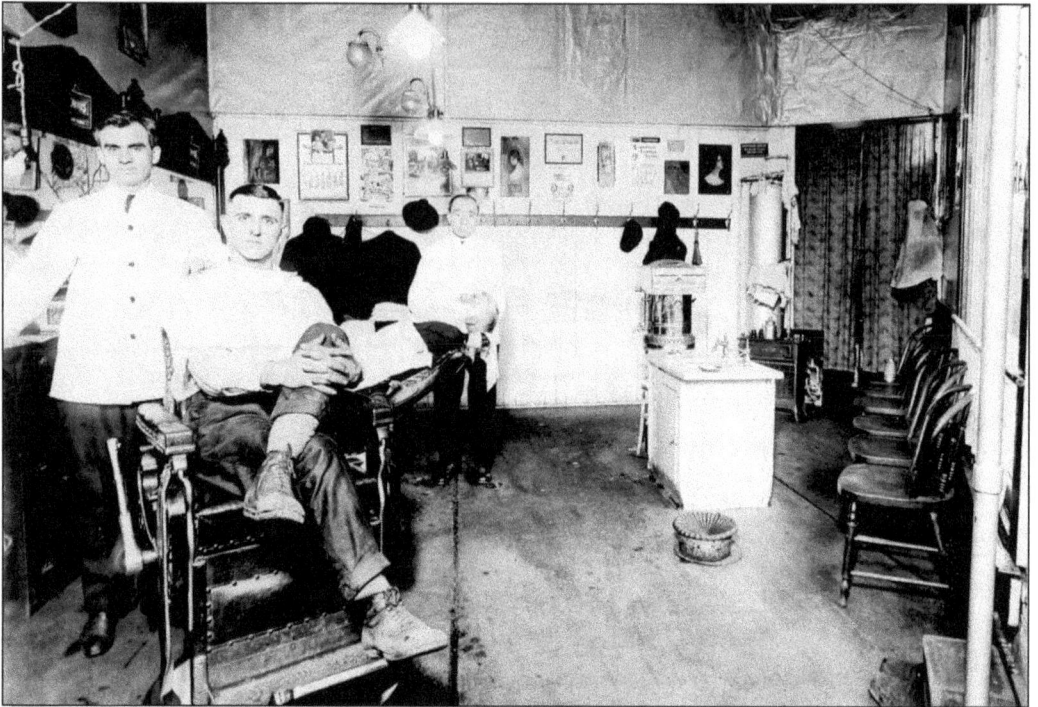

In an interior view of the Ceplecha Barbershop, James Ceplecha (left) and his brother Joseph (back right) take a break from cutting the hair of unidentified customers to pose for the picture. This photograph is a rare interior view and vintage photograph of a bygone era.

The post office was located in this building during the early part of the 20th century and was used until the 1970s when it was bought by a private citizen. In 2006, the Dunbar Historical Society purchased the building, which now houses the society's education center and archives.

Three

TRAGEDIES

This sketch is an eyewitness account drawn by A. E. Harbaugh, known as the "Mountain Poet," shortly after the 1890 Hill Farm Mine explosion that killed 31 miners. This view of the site shows the location of the pit mouth and the workings at the mine, owned by the Dunbar Furnace Company at the time of the tragedy. (Courtesy of George R. and Donna R. Myers.)

One of Dunbar's most tragic accidents occurred on June 16, 1890, when the Hill Farm Mine explosion killed 31 workers. The photograph, from the 1890 *Reports of Inspectors of Coal Mines* book, shows the conflagration rising on the left and the spectators on the right perched on the fence high above the man way to the mine. Rescue efforts lasted 16 days, and access to the workers was attempted through the Mahoning Mine. After several days, with rescuers realizing the maps were not correct and ending up some distance away from their intended destination, the mine was sealed and all hope was lost to save the miners. In March 1892, the bodies were removed from the mine. In November 1903, an explosion in the adjacent Ferguson Mine killed 18 men. According to a 1921 news article, the remains of Mike Benny were found 18 years after the explosion. Turning left instead of right, Benny became trapped in the room that would be his tomb for 18 years.

Using oil crayon and India ink, A. E. Harbaugh drew this sketch of the steam fan at the man way of the Mahoning Mine around 1890. This mine was located a short distance from the Hill Farm Mine. A self-taught artist from Mill Run, Harbaugh was referred to by the Uniontown *Genius of Liberty* and the Connellsville *Courier* as a "young and rising artist." (Courtesy of George R. and Donna R. Myers.)

This photograph, from the 1890 *Reports of Inspectors of Coal Mines* book, shows the Mahoning Mine, which had 100 coke ovens in 1875. The works was located off Ranch Road in Dunbar. The mine was often idle due to water in the dip workings. It was through this mine attempts were made to rescue workers involved in the Hill Farm explosion. The ovens exist today in various states of disrepair.

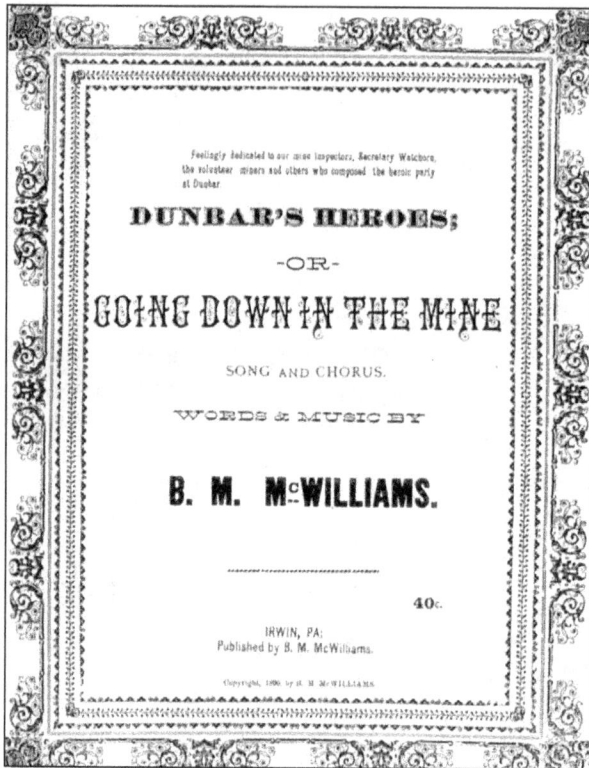

Feelingly dedicated to our mine inspectors, Secretary Watchorn, the volunteer miners and others who composed the heroic party at Dunbar

DUNBAR'S HEROES;

-OR-

GOING DOWN IN THE MINE

SONG AND CHORUS.

WORDS & MUSIC BY

B. M. McWILLIAMS.

40c.

IRWIN, PA;
Published by B. M. McWilliams.

Copyright, 1890, by B. M. McWILLIAMS

So great was the 1890 tragedy at the Hill Farm Mine that B. M. McWilliams wrote the song "Dunbar's Heroes; or Going Down in the Mine." He dedicated the song to those men who tried so valiantly to save the workers trapped in the mine after the explosion. One of those souls lost in the mine was John Kopf Cope (below, center), a veteran of the Civil War. Along with 29 others, Cope and his young son Andrew were killed in that terrible explosion. It was not uncommon for sons to work with their fathers in order to learn how to mine and to bring in some extra income. When a disaster like this struck, families often suffered double losses, as happened with the Cope family. (Left, courtesy of George R. and Donna R. Myers; below, courtesy of Carmella Hardy.)

This 1907 flood photograph shows a view taken south of Dunbar as the waters of Dunbar Creek rushed toward the town. The Bryson Hill area of Dunbar is seen in the top area of the photograph, while Short Street is visible below. Damage was severe to the buildings that lined the creek. (Courtesy of George R. and Donna R. Myers.)

This company house, owned by the Dunbar Furnace Company, is shown shortly after the 1912 flood. The creek, between the company houses and the furnace, flowed high in the narrow hollow as the flood headed to Dunbar. This area of town was called Feathers Row after I. N. Feathers. It was a heavily traveled area for people who headed toward their homes on Furnace Hill and the Dunbar Mountains.

One victim of Dunbar's 1912 flood was the Burhans Funeral Home block. The water completely washed out the corner foundation of the building, and workers tried to shore it up to avoid collapse. The signs for the Burhans funeral director and the waiting room of the West Penn Railways Company can be seen farther down the block. (Courtesy of George R. and Donna R. Myers.)

This 1912 photograph shows a view of the northern area of town near the Dunbar Post Office. The crushed building in the center is the remains of Kelly's Jewelry Store, which came to rest across from the post office several blocks from its original location. The Pennsylvania Railroad platform was not severely damaged, and it provided a vantage point for people to inspect the harm caused by the raging waters.

50

These two Dunbar scenes speak volumes about the severity of the flood that ravaged Dunbar in 1912. Water rolling down from the mountains inundated the town, and Dunbar Creek and Gist Run overflowed their banks. In the photograph above, looking north, the Pennsylvania Railroad station is seen at left; the Muscenti stables and debris caught by the bridge are seen on the right. Below is the same view looking south. The railroad tracks can be seen at right with all the roadbed gone. In the center, a displaced building sits on the main street bridge with a roof on the right. (Courtesy of George R. and Donna R. Myers.)

Water pours over Connellsville and Woodvale Streets and back into Dunbar Creek during the 1954 flood. The corner of the Central Drugstore is seen on the left. The drugstore was built to withstand the water of Dunbar Creek, which ran adjacent to the foundation of the building.

Known far and wide to shoppers seeking a bargain, Pechin Shopping Village was a landmark in Dunbar for more than 50 years. Started by Sullivan D'Amico in 1947, Pechin's fame was due to its great values, like 19¢ hamburgers. The renowned shopping destination with some buildings constructed over Dunbar Creek met its demise on June 9, 2006, when a devastating fire destroyed the entire complex.

Four

TRANSPORTATION

Dunbar's history is closely tied to the coming of the railroads and the trolleys. The railroads provided jobs to the locals, and the trolleys increased mobility for residents. The New Haven and Dunbar Railroad was a short line that operated to meet the needs of the iron industry in Dunbar. Workers are, from left to right, Charlie Hawk, Biddie Doyle, Russ Brubaker, and unidentified. (Courtesy of Arnold and Phyllis Brubaker.)

These vintage photographs show two of the New Haven and Dunbar Railroad engines. Above is the New Haven and Dunbar Railroad engine No. 12. The three men in the photograph are unidentified. The engine appears new and may have just been put into service. The date is unknown. Below is the New Haven and Dunbar Railroad engine No. 15. Trainmen shown are, from left to right, Ed Brubaker, Al Gray, unidentified, and Denny Lancaster. (Courtesy of Arnold and Phyllis Brubaker.)

The Baldwin engine (above) and the Whitcomb war surplus engine (below) were two of the last engines operated by the New Haven and Dunbar Railroad. Started in 1879 with 5,300 feet of track, the railroad had 7 locomotives, 39 coal cars, 6 track cars, and a little over 13 miles of track by 1911. The Dunbar Furnace Company entered receivership in 1911, and the American Manganese Company succeeded the furnace company and inherited the railroad. In 1924, the Dunbar Corporation was formed to continue operation of the sand mill. Over the years, the number of engines was reduced to two and finally one. The line depended on the bluestone quarry until it closed in 1949. The closing of the sand mill in 1954 sealed the railroad's fate, and it closed in 1955. (Courtesy of Arnold and Phyllis Brubaker.)

A favorite gathering place for the men of Dunbar was the Baltimore and Ohio Railroad station. The photograph above from about 1909 shows the third station built since the opening of the railroad during the winter of 1859–1860. Originally, a small flag station was located near Speers Mill, and around 1866, a small station was built where the one pictured was located. This larger station was later built to handle the increased amount of freight. The photograph below shows the Pennsylvania Railroad station. This track was completed in 1876, and a small station was built. Soon after, this larger station was constructed to handle the ever-increasing use of train travel. Riders can be seen leaving the station. The track has now been converted to the Sheepskin Trail. Both stations were torn down in the 1950s or early 1960s.

This photograph shows the Pennsylvania Railroad station in the center and the post office building on the right. On the left, part of a boxcar can be seen on the siding that once existed at the station. The railroad track, now the Sheepskin Trail, is the first spur off the Great Allegheny Passage, which runs between Washington, D. C., and Pittsburgh.

Bowest Restaurant, known locally as the Beanery, was a restaurant and train facility owned by the Western Maryland Railroad. In addition to being used as a restaurant by locals, rooms were available for use by trainmen who had to stay overnight between runs. Over the years, managers included Adolph and Ginny Tristani and Harold and Katie Harvey. The building has been torn down. (Courtesy of Arnold and Phyllis Brubaker.)

One of the last steam engines to use the line is shown steaming toward H. P. Smith Meat Market. Only the width of a sidewalk separates the store from the moving train. A man who appears to be taking photographs can be seen on the sidewalk waiting for the train to arrive. Another coal train is seen at the right in the photograph.

These employees sit on a Western Maryland Railroad engine while they pose for this photograph. On the far right is John R. Ziska; all others are unidentified. The Western Maryland Railroad provided locals with jobs for many years before operations left Dunbar. At one time, three tracks were needed to handle the number of trains traveling through Dunbar.

The "New Haven" in New Haven and Dunbar Railroad was the west side of Connellsville, where the line was surveyed to go but was never built. The railroad became a wholly owned subsidiary of Dunbar Furnace Company in 1892 after operating as a plant railroad since 1879. The only passengers that the train ever carried were Sunday school picnickers who rode flatcars to the Betty Knox area in the Dunbar Mountains.

At right is Art McCormick (1876–1932), shown after he lost his leg. He worked for the Baltimore and Ohio Railroad in 1906 as a brakeman. While checking a coupling, he slipped under the wheels of a train. Three days later, his replacement suffered the same fate. The unidentified man (left) also lost his leg in a train accident. Both posed for this unique photograph. (Courtesy of Jerry and Christine Ryan.)

A West Penn trolley begins its climb up the long trestle that will take it over the Bowest yards. The huge wooden structure was built when the trolley first came to Dunbar in June 1903. Through service to Uniontown started in July 1903. The West Penn Railways Company was formed by the merger of two companies in March 1905, and Dunbar's love affair with the bright orange trolley began.

This photograph of the trolley crossing the high, wooden trestle shows a view of the Bowest yards below. Rail workers stop to watch the big orange car as it passes overhead, always a sight to see. For all the mobility that the trolley afforded residents, it was not without its accidents. Through the years, many people were maimed and killed while working for the company or walking on the rails.

So common was the sight of the trolley on "Brick Hill" that even this boy stops his bicycle just short of the rails to let the trolley pass. The trolley made its way through town, following Connellsville Street and Woodvale Street to points south including Shady Grove. First known as Trolley Park, it was built to help increase ridership on the line in the early years of the trolley.

This West Penn trolley can be seen at the bottom of the Church Hill area of Dunbar. The trolley line ran parallel to the two railroad tracks on the left in the photograph. These tracks provided a quick walk to the Pechin area, but this was the location of several trolley accidents.

All good things must come to an end, and for the West Penn Railways Company trolley, it happened on August 11, 1952. Residents decided to give the trolley a proper burial by chartering a special car and having a wake at the Connellsville and Uniontown end of the ride. Above is the crowd of around 75 mourners who rode this special trolley, including Congressman Edward Sittler. A small banner-draped coffin was provided by local undertaker J. T. Burhans (front, far right), and it was carried by pallbearers in swallowtailed coats. Pictured behind the coffin are, from left to right, Max Martin, Wayne Watson Sr., Gerald Rossi, and J. P. Miller. Mourners arriving at each destination got off the trolley and paraded the little coffin around the terminal complete with requiem music. Below is the ticket that was required for the last regular trolley run.

WEST PENN RAILWAYS CO.

FINAL TRIP OF YOUR FAMILIAR TROLLEY
LAST RUN
Connellsville — South Connellsville — Dunbar — Uniontown
11:15 P. M., South Connellsville   11:30 P. M., Connellsville   Saturday, August 9, 1952

Substituted Bus Service
BY
FAYETTE COACH LINES
Beginning Sunday, August 10, 1952

GUEST

PLEASE SHOW TO OPERATOR

Five

LOCAL FOLKS AND
COLORFUL CHARACTERS

As with all small towns, Dunbar is made up of common folks whose dedication and love of the community through the years have helped to make it a great place to live. Many have served in a variety of ways. There are also those colorful characters like Ground Hog Sam—his real name forgotten—whose eccentric personalities have impacted the community and created some special memories for local folks.

The Thomas T. Morrison family has deep roots in the Dunbar community. Pictured are Thomas T. Morrison (1868–1957) and Bertha J. Bodkin Morrison (1873–1932) with twins Olga (left) and Omar, sitting between their parents, and son Robert R. Morrison (back), who became one of Dunbar's doctors. Thomas T. Morrison taught for many years in Dunbar area schools. An educated man, he accepted a job with the Semet-Solvay Company counting bricks, which resulted in a pay increase. An aging Thomas T. Morrison (below, center) is seen visiting his grandsons Dennis Morrison (left) and Donald Morrison, who, years later, was instrumental in publishing *Dunbar: The Furnace Town*, a 1983 centennial publication. (Courtesy of Dennis Morrison.)

Dr. Robert R. Morrison (1894–1959) was born in Wharton Township. A 1912 graduate of Connellsville High School, he attended Jefferson Medical School and graduated in 1920. As a first sergeant of the Reserve Officers' Training Corps (ROTC) during World War I, his class was leaving for the war zone when word came that the war had ended. (Courtesy of Dennis Morrison.)

Large families were not uncommon in Dunbar, and the Fitzgeralds were no exception. They were a hardworking Dunbar family whose home was located on what is now Memorial Street. Shown are, from left to right, (first row) Margaret, Maurice, Edward, Mary, Michael, and Martha; (second row) John, Victoria Daley Fitzgerald (mother), Michael J. Fitzgerald (father), William, and Daniel. (Courtesy of the Fitzgerald family.)

Ex-slave John Craig was born in 1845 on a plantation near Odessa, Maryland. Due to a caring plantation owner, he gained an early education. After the Civil War, he found his way to Dunbar where he worked for the American Manganese Company and the First National Bank. He was best known for his "black philosophy and praises of President Lincoln." His greatest desire in life was to meet Abraham Lincoln. Married three times, he had no children, and according to the February 12, 1938, *Morning Herald*, "He lived out his days in Dunbar having lived through the administrations of 22 presidents." No date of death is known, but he was 93 years old at the time of the 1938 newspaper article.

Emma Catharine Wishart Rechenberg (1912–2003), daughter of Andrew and Florence Wishart, holds her beautiful vintage doll as she poses for this picture. Her family owned the Dunbar Bakery. Baptized in 1913, she was a member in the Dunbar Presbyterian Church for 91 years. She was a registered nurse, married Paul Rechenberg, and had four children, Margaret, Paul, Rick, and June Ann. (Courtesy of the Rechenberg family.)

This vintage photograph shows Robert Dunaway enjoying his classy new pedal car. A car of this caliber was a very unique vehicle for a child in Dunbar, and it was the pride of any youngster who owned it. Making sure he remains safe is Mary Dunaway, who looks on as he takes a spin around his yard. (Courtesy of Donna Murray.)

Clowning around in this posed photograph are, from left to right, Joseph D. Morrison (1863–1952) and Thomas T. Morrison (1868–1957). The original picture is a tintype made using the daguerreotype process invented in 1839 by Frenchman Louis J. M. Daguerre (1789–1851). Thomas T. Morrison taught for many years in the Dunbar schools. (Courtesy of Dennis Morrison.)

Ellen Smitley, known as the "snake lady" or "snake charmer," moved from the Dunbar Mountains and lived at the bottom of Church Hill. Some folks found her a little eccentric because she had some unusual pets, like monkeys, rats, snakes, and boa constrictors. After the death of her pets, it is said that they were stuffed and placed around the family home in the mountains. (Courtesy of Angela Cooper.)

Driving around Dunbar in his roadster is Dr. Edwin B. Guie. He provided medical services to the townsfolk between 1910 and 1942. His longevity in town made him one of Dunbar's most recognized faces. His office was located on Railroad Street, where Dr. Robert Guie later took over the practice. Still standing, the building is currently used for apartments.

Dr. W. J. Hamilton sits in front of his Dunbar home and office on Church Street. Hamilton came to Dunbar in the spring of 1873 and served the area until 1910. His horse and buggy was a familiar sight as he went about taking care of the medical needs of Dunbar's families. Built in 1982, the current post office building is located on the site of Hamilton's office.

Originally from Ohio, J. N. Burhans, grandfather of Louise Burhans (left) and Florentz Todd Burhans (right), came to Dunbar in 1902 and operated a funeral home and livery stable. Upon his death, his son J. T. Burhans came from California in 1918 to obtain his funeral director's license and take over his father's business. Florentz Todd Burhans took over the funeral home in 1946 after his tour of duty in the armed forces. He and his wife, Mary Ellen Burhans, were very active in both business and civic activities in Dunbar and were members of the Dunbar Presbyterian Church. Mary Catherine Reed (below, left) and Todd Burhans (below, right) watch one of Dunbar's Memorial Day parades. (Courtesy of George R. and Donna R. Myers.)

George Trimbath (1913–1974) is shown delivering milk door-to-door in the Dunbar area. Well known around town, he was a civic-minded resident who served on the honor roll committee, was president of the Dunbar Volunteer Fire Company for more than 20 years, and served on the Dunbar Borough Council. He was honored as Dunbar's Man of the Year in 1973.

Chef Harold "Baron" Galand (1928–1992) began his career at 13 in the kitchen of the Lazy Hour Ranch. He went on to become the coach of the United States Culinary Olympic Team. His accomplishments and awards are too numerous to mention. When he was inducted into the Chefs Hall of Fame, he remarked, "We may live without birds, trees and books but civilized man can never live without cooks!"

The 1954 flood did not spare the Nick Bell Store, located on Connellsville Street. Debris can be seen in the parking area, and the fire department had to remove water from the basement of the store. Started in 1942 by Nick Bell Sr., the store was renowned for its fresh-cut meat and produce. A friendly face, Bell welcomed everyone to the store and often cashed payroll checks for his customers while extending credit so families could eat until payday. Bell (below, left) and store butcher Harry Selby (right) make sausage by hand in the store for shoppers. It was one of Dunbar's most well-patronized grocery stores and certainly one with a heart. (Above, courtesy of Mary D. Ryan; below, courtesy of Nick Bell Jr.)

William "Bump" Martin, known as Charles Atlas, stands in front of Rose Ann's Candy Kitchen, owned by Rose Ann Giampetro. The store, located in the Smith building across from the Baltimore and Ohio Railroad station, holds strong memories for many residents. Folks remember Giampetro having a jukebox and holding dances. The most vivid memories are of the homemade chocolate candy and double-scooped ice-cream cones. (Courtesy of Doris Lizza.)

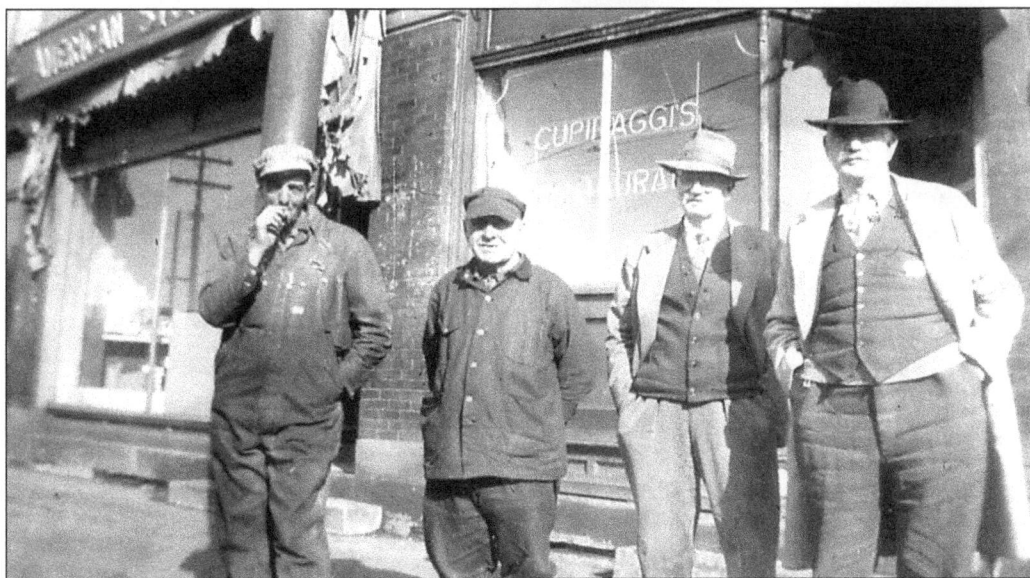

Located in the First National Bank building, the American Store and Cupiraggi's Restaurant can be seen in the background of this photograph. Home to several different stores and bars through the years, it was a gathering place for Dunbar locals. Shown are, from left to right, Walter McManus, Jake Warman, W. G. Hay, and George Hostetler.

This photograph was taken in 1946, the year that Elaine Quairiere (Pecil) (left) and Josephine Caruso (McCune) (right) graduated from Dunbar Township High School. In the center is Doris Spangler (Harvey), who graduated in 1947. According to Harvey, this photograph was taken as these young ladies were "just walking around the big city of Dunbar."

Charles (Charlie) Spangler (1902–1979) came to Dunbar in 1929 to work on the railroad. He married Florence Suder, and they had two children, Charles, who died at age 10, and Doris. Active in community work, he was Dunbar's Man of the Year in 1977. On the left are American Legion Hughes Post No. 146 members James Hardy (with trumpet), Louis Ross (center), and Albert DeMott (right). Others are unidentified. (Courtesy of George R. and Donna R. Myers.)

One of Dunbar's favorite sons is state senator J. William Lincoln, born in October 1940. His political career began with his election as district justice in 1970. He served in the Pennsylvania House of Representatives from 1973 to 1978, when he was elected state senator. He served for 16 years in that role.

Enjoying a rest in downtown Dunbar is Ewing Marcus Marietta (1904–1964). He was married to Irene Marietta, a correspondent for the local newspaper for many years. His brother Jay Donald Marietta owned Marietta's Store, which was formerly located where the Dunbar House once stood. Ewing worked for his brother operating a truck and hauling coal for the state. (Courtesy of Jon Marietta.)

Famous as the founder of Pechin Shopping Village, Sullivan D'Amico (1917–2005) was also a philanthropist, quietly helping people in need without desire of recognition. In 1947, the first Pechin store was opened in his home before moving down the street where more stores were added. His business savvy and low prices landed him on the front page of the *Wall Street Journal* in 1984 and three times in the *National Enquirer*. Below is a view of Pechin Shopping Village before the 2006 fire that destroyed the entire complex. The complex housed a grocery store, deli, shoe store, drugstore, bakery, clothing store, sporting goods store, farm store, department store, and beer distributor. Out-of-state people frequented the complex as often as the locals.

Council members pictured here between 1959 and 1961 are, from left to right, (first row) Paul Mahoney, Hugh Dunaway, Paul Fitzgerald, and Jerry Rossi; (second row) Lawrence Bruno, Greek Bruno, George Trimbath, Wayne Watson Sr., Jack Kline, and Chris Hughes. The Dunbar Borough Council chambers were and still are located in the Central Bank building, a structure with unique architectural appointments and shape.

Three pillars of the Dunbar community relax after taking part in the dedication of the Dunbar Historical Society center in 2006. From left to right are former mayor Warne Rankin, Dunbar councilman William Watson, and Mayor John C. Williams. All have dedicated their time and energy to making Dunbar a better place to live. Watson will be fondly remembered for his love of Dunbar. (Courtesy of Michael J. Bell.)

The legend goes that Betty Knox, born in 1842, lived on a farm at Kentuck Knob overlooking Ohiopyle. When she was three, her mother died, and she was reared by her father. She quickly learned to do chores beyond her years. Her father died when she was 19, and she had to make a living for herself. She hauled grain on an ox from her home to the gristmill near Ferguson Valley. She placed stones to create a small spring where she stopped on her way to and from the mill. She took the same route every day, and an area along Dunbar Creek is known as Betty Knox. Her trips along the mountain continued until 1878, when she failed to show up on her daily trek. In 1879, the skeleton of her ox was found tied to a tree near the spring, but she was never found. The mystery of Betty Knox has fascinated people for decades. Robert Melvin Martin, a lifelong resident of Irishtown, near Dunbar, paid tribute to her story by drawing this picture of Betty Knox from an oral history.

Six

PATRIOTISM AND FAITH

Dunbar's military heritage includes patriots who have served in all conflicts since the Revolutionary War. These boots and the poem penned by V. V. Scott reflect the pride and heartfelt compassion of a mother whose son took part in the war effort. Through the years, the strong foundation of faith shown by Dunbar's residents has brought strength and solace to believers.

Merry Xmas 1939

The Mother and The Soldier who wore these shoes in the World's War hope that all shoes may walk in the Path of Peace

Dec. 25 - 1939

The Soldier - W. P. Scott
The Mother - V. V. Scott

The greatest visible expression of Dunbar's love of country is the beautiful Dunbar Honor Roll (above). After a civilian defense meeting in 1942, it was suggested that Dunbar should have a memorial as a lasting expression of the regard of the citizenry for those who so valiantly served in the armed forces. The result was the formation of the Victory Park Association. On a bluff above town, the site of the former Fairview School was chosen as the location. The deed cost $1, and both Dunbar Township and Dunbar Borough School District gave a share of the property. Volunteers completed 75 percent of the labor. The people (below) who completed much of the masonry work are, from left to right, George Hostetler, Jack Hughes, unidentified, and John Azariah Lehman.

Almost everyone in town showed up for the departure of the men and women who left from Dunbar during World War II. In this picture, the West Penn trolley picks up the soldiers in front of the Burhans Funeral Home. While the pride in the community was evident during the event, parents and friends were sad to see them leave.

Joseph Cortese was a prisoner of war during World War II. A paratrooper, he was captured during the invasion of Normandy on June 9, 1944. After the war ended, Cortese returned home in 1946 and married Madelyn Zammarelli. They had two children, Joseph and Diane. His parents, Salvatore and Caroline Cortese, had seven children, all who served in the armed forces during World War II.

Lt. Walter Curtis Carr (left), copilot of a Flying Fortress in World War II, was killed in November 1943 during his 13th combat mission, a daylight bomb raid on Gelsenkirchen, Germany. He was a member of the 8th Army Air Corps stationed in Ridgewell, England, and he enlisted in 1942. His remains were never found. In 1969, during dredging operations in the Diep River in Holland, Carr's dog tags were found along with parts of the plane. He was the son of Herman and Margaret Lehman Carr and a 1939 graduate of Dunbar Township High School. Recognition of his service and sacrifice is engraved on the wall of the Court of Honor in the Netherlands American Cemetery in Margraten, Netherlands. On October 7, 2007, a memorial stone (below), provided by the U.S. Department of Veterans Affairs, was placed in Mount Auburn Cemetery to honor Carr. (Courtesy of Curtis Lehman.)

Born on July 24, 1838, Francis C. Wilhelm (right) fought in the Civil War in 1861 with the Ohio Regiment and used the Spencer repeating rifle. He died on October 16, 1914, and is buried in the Dickerson Run Cemetery. His wife, Mary Jane Tissue Wilhelm, was born on July 26, 1841, and died on May 29, 1920. Carrie Wilhelm (below) was a well-known face around Dunbar. Born in 1896, she was a seamstress in town and was highly regarded by the residents. She was a member of the Dunbar Baptist Church on Speers Hill where she taught Sunday school. Her home on Woodvale Street was one of Dunbar's most quaint houses. She died in 1984. (Courtesy of Carmella Hardy.)

Pictured dressed in his World War I uniform, Richard Harvey Jr. was born in 1892. After returning from the service, he married Mary Josephine Bereiter and they had four children, Florence, Richard, Charles, and Mary Margaret. He died on March 9, 1966. His son Charles, who served in World War II, passed away exactly 31 years later on March 9, 1997. Both are buried at Mount Auburn Cemetery. (Courtesy of George R. and Donna R. Myers.)

Shown in his World War II uniform is Coburn H. Tressler (1909–1954). The Tressler family owned the old Hughes farm on the Dunbar-Ohiopyle Road, where Tressler is buried. It was common for families to have small family cemeteries located on their property. Through the efforts of Lanny Golden and others, the cemetery project has located and photographed the cemeteries and headstones in Fayette County.

Dearl J. "Bud" Lowry, son of Solon and Blanche Russell Lowry, was born in November 1917. Lowry proudly served his country in the U.S. Navy for two years and the U.S. Army for 20 years. The recipient of the Medal of Honor and Bronze Star, he served in World War II, the Korean War, and two tours of duty in the Vietnam conflict. He died in January 2007.

William (Bill) Rockwell was a man for all seasons. He proudly served his country during World War II. As an artist, he excelled with his pen-and-ink drawings and oil paintings, two of which are on display at the Dunbar Historical Society. He served his community by working throughout his lifetime with the Boy Scout troops and was one of the Dunbar Historical Society's founding members.

Former mayor Angela Graziano shows her patriotic spirit on Memorial Day in 2007. Elected the first woman mayor in 1977, she campaigned for a "clean sweep" for Dunbar. After being sworn in, she could be seen around town with a broom in her hand, sweeping the streets to fulfill her campaign promise. She was instrumental in starting a community Christmas party for children and proudly marched in Dunbar's parades.

Sitting in front of the beautiful Dunbar Honor Roll are Oliver Wayne Martin (left) and Robert Melvin Martin. The brothers, who served their country during World War II, were knighted into the French Legion of Honor on September 29, 2007. The award is France's highest honor given for outstanding service to France during World War II. Jean-Pierre Collet, the French consul general for western Pennsylvania, conducted the knighting ceremony.

Built in 1881, St. John's in the Wilderness Episcopal Church (right) is located near the Furnace School. The first Episcopalian worshippers met in Edmund Pechin's home until the church was built. The church closed in the 1970s. The stained glass, altar ware, and bell were moved to Christ Episcopal Church in Brownsville. The church was sold and remodeled and is now a home (left) that is still in use.

Wesley Methodist Church, formerly called the Methodist Episcopal Church, appears today as it did when it was dedicated in 1903. The land was purchased from William Dull after the building that had occupied the property burned down. Originally, members met at various locations until a frame church was built on Woodvale Street in 1887. Later sold, it burned down in 1902. (Courtesy of John and Bonnie Zurick Jr.)

Organized as the result of a series of evangelistic meetings, Dunbar Baptist Church first held services at the Harper's School. In 1888, Rev. J. R. Brown was called as the first pastor, and in 1892, the cornerstone for the church on Speers Hill was laid with the building dedication held in 1894. Services are still conducted in the church today. The Faith Baptist Church (not shown) started in 1968 when meetings were held in various homes, the Lions Club, and the Odd Fellows hall. In 1969, the congregation broke ground for a church building on land donated by the Lloyd Williams family. The church, located a short distance outside Dunbar on Ferguson Road, is still active in the community.

Located a short distance from town, Pechin Community Chapel remains an active family of faith in the Dunbar community. The land was laid out by A. W. Bliss, and in 1906, a tract was given to David Foltz and Frank McFarland. McFarland deeded his share to Foltz in the same year, and it was designated that the land was to be used for religious purposes only. Some leading citizens of the community banded together to form the church and laid the cornerstone for the old Pechin Community Chapel on Ferguson Road. During a 2003 renovation project, the cornerstone was uncovered. Inside were six newspapers dated February 27, 1909, a Bible with the names of the founding members, and two pennies dated 1880. (Courtesy of Pastor Lee Maley.)

The Franklin Memorial United Methodist Church (above) is one of the oldest Methodist churches in the Connellsville district. The congregation worshipped at various locations before building this church in 1875. The original entrance faced Woodvale Street as shown in the photograph. When a Sunday school was added, the entrance was moved to face Bridge Street. In 1887, Rev. W. H. Gladden was very successful in building new churches and starting young men out in the ministry. His son Rev. T. M. Gladden was pastor at the church in 1912. The Franklin Methodist group picture below was taken at the Williams farm between 1890 and 1910. The Williams farm, between Cowrock and River Hill, was a favorite picnic area in the late 1800s. Today the church remains active in the Dunbar community.

St. Aloysius Church (above), first located on Church Hill, had a rectory, church, school, and convent. The first mass was held in 1869 at a stone house south of the Church Hill property. The first service in the church, built in 1875, was held with no pews. Fr. Arthur Devlin came to the parish in 1881, and under his watch, plans were made for a church cemetery. In July 1887, Devlin died suddenly and was the first and only priest buried at the cemetery. The school and convent were built in 1887. The school closed in 1964. The crowning of the May queen celebration (below) was held in 1937. Elma Panone Marzano (front, center) was crowned queen and Joan M. Graziano (front, left of queen) was the ring bearer. In 1967, the church purchased the Lazy Hour Ranch property and built a new church.

When the first railroad reached Dunbar, there were only three Presbyterian families who lived in town, including those of Joseph Paull, James McDowell, and Thomas Watt. They rented a handcar and went to church in Connellsville until 1870, when the "church train" was chartered for $7.50 per day. Riders from all denominations could use the train and pay half fare to attend churches in Connellsville. In 1873, full fare was demanded by the railroad, but the riders refused to pay, so the train was discontinued. Watt donated the land for a new church (above), and it was built in 1874. It was the first church built in Dunbar. The church was raised to add a basement in 1924, and the doors in the picture above are now second-story windows. The picture of the church picnic below shows fun and games at Shady Grove Park.

Seven

SCHOOLS AND ORGANIZATIONS

The Harper's School, built in the late 1800s, was known as the stone schoolhouse. When interviewed in 1965, James Bailes remembered attending the school in 1891. In 1929, the school became the meeting hall for Boy Scout Troop 1-180. Over the years, the Scouts have maintained the building, and it is still in use today as their meeting hall and looks much the same as it originally appeared. (Courtesy of Dearl Lowry.)

The vintage photograph above shows the students at the stone Dunbar Borough School located on Connellsville Street sometime between 1870 and 1892. John Anderson (back, in front of left window) was the teacher. Bertha J. Bodkin (right of Anderson) went on to become a teacher at the Fayette School. The stone building was torn down to make room for the Dunbar Borough School (below), which operated from 1892 to 1974. The school remained in use as an educational facility for a few years after the school district closed the building. It is currently used for storage. Opened in 1975, the current Dunbar Borough School is located behind Laurel Mall. (Courtesy of Dennis Morrison.)

Named the Fairview School because there was a "fair view" of town from its location on the hill overlooking Dunbar, this school is now the location of the beautiful Dunbar Honor Roll in Memorial Park. The school burned down, and the stone from the building was used in the construction of the honor roll. No additional information is known about this school or the names of the students.

This 1895 teacher institute notice invites teachers and the public to take part in an event that included sessions on duties of parents, good citizenship, and preparation of lessons. The notice states that the Dunbar Normal School would open on May 6, 1895, and there was "no better training school in the country." A staunch supporter of education, J. S. Carroll was the principal. (Courtesy of Dennis Morrison.)

TEACHERS' INSTITUTE,

TO BE HELD AT_____

DUNBAR. PENN'A.,
Saturday, Jan. 12, 1895.

Forenoon Session at 10 A. M.
MUSIC.

School Addresses	O. P. Moser, Rev. W. G. Stewart
Duties of Parents	C. S. Smith
Preparation of Lessons	W. S. Bryan
Address	G. B. Jeffries

Afternoon Session at 1 P. M.
MUSIC.

Good Citizenship	A. J. Gans
Defects in Teaching	R. V. Ritenour
Words—Words—Words	Wooda Carr
Address	Dr. T. N. Boyle

MUSIC.

Thorough Work	J. G. Carroll
Public Days	Ira L. Smith
Home Study	J. M. Murtland
Address	W. G. Gans

MUSIC.

J. B. Meese, W. H. Cooke, L. M. Herrington, R. F. Hopwood, W. B. McCollough, Lee Smith, W. D. McGinnis, H. S. Dumbauld, W. E. Crow, and other prominent educators will be with us.
Teachers and friends of education are invited.
J. S. CARROLL, Principal.

N. B.---The Dunbar Normal School will open May 6th. No better training school in the country. Special attention given to Arithmetic, Grammar and Theory.

Part of the Dunbar Township school system, Fayette School No. 1 (not shown) operated from 1889 to 1919, and Fayette School No. 2 (above) operated from 1919 to 1947. Fayette School No. 1 was located on York Street, and Fayette School No. 2 was on Connellsville Street. Bertha J. Bodkin, a teacher at this school, was a member of Dunbar Borough High School's first graduating class in 1891. Today both schools are private residences. (Courtesy of Dennis Morrison.)

Built in 1888, Gettemy School was located on the old Jumonville Road between Irishtown and Old Braddock Road. Silas Gettemy donated the land. This photograph shows the one-story single-room school that was also referred to as Hog Rocks School. Robert M. Martin reports that his mother, Agnes McClane, attended school there. The building is now privately owned and being restored.

Born in 1915, Robert C. Hughes went to the Hughes School located on Tucker Run Road off the Dunbar-Ohiopyle Road. The one-room school was heated by a potbellied stove, and children all drank water from the same tin dipper. According to Hughes, teacher Harry Crouse had a wooden paddle that sat next to the blackboard, and he used it often. John L. Golden (1889–1969) also taught at the Hughes School.

Liston School, located near Kingan Hill off Camp Carmel Road, operated in the mid-1900s. Joseph W. "Buck" Martin attended this school in 1944. In addition to Martin, there were eight students at that time, Wilbur Murphy, Shirley Roebuck, Leona Roebuck, Ernestine Martin, Glenn Martin, James Savalas, George Roebuck, and John Roebuck. The teacher was A. E. Crouse. The building has since been torn down. (Courtesy of Joseph W. Martin.)

Like a sentinel keeping watch over town, the Odd Fellows hall (above) was located on Speers Hill. The King David Lodge No. 826, Independent Order of Odd Fellows was organized in 1873 with 23 members. During the 14th and 15th centuries in small towns and villages, there were not enough men from the same trade to set up a local guild. So men from a number of trades formed a group of fellows from an odd assortment of trades. Hence, the name Odd Fellows came into use. A familiar sight for decades, sitting on the crest of the hill, the three-story Odd Fellows building was used for many functions and in later years housed apartments. To many people's dismay, the building was torn down (left) in September 1978. (Courtesy of Diana Homer.)

American Legion Hughes Post No. 146 was organized in May 1924. Meeting at various locations in town, it purchased the Foltz property in 1939. The 1952 officers are, from left to right, (first row) Anthony Maddas, Comdr. Robert Martin, and Todd Burhans; (second row) Altha Bodkin, Roy Hardy, Martin Buzzelli, Calvin Rockwell, and Christopher Hughes. Reaching its peak membership in 1946 with 284 members, the organization remains active today. (Courtesy of Robert M. Martin.)

Organized in 1924, the American Legion Hughes Post No. 146 Ladies Auxiliary supported the community by sponsoring Memorial Day programs, Christmas food baskets, Easter egg hunts, and Scout and baseball activities. Members of the auxiliary are, from left to right, (first row) Effie Hughes, unidentified, Isabelle Clements, and Jean Trenker; (second row) Della Jeffries, Henrietta Hardy, Ann Topper, Mae Hardy, and Lucy Roebuck. (Courtesy of the Christopher Hughes family.)

The Dunbar Township High School marching band is shown between 1945 and 1950 at the Dunbar Township stadium located at Trotter. Wallace Smiley, who played the saxophone, was a band member in 1946 and 1947. He recalls the band playing for many events, including parades, football games, and concerts at East Park in Connellsville. (Courtesy of the Cross family.)

In January 1975, the Dunbar Community Center Mini-Project Committee opened the Dunbar Library, a branch of Carnegie Free Library. Committee members were Harold Dunaway, John Connors, Shirley Szabo, Reba Zeikus, Alice Nebraska, Mary Ellen Burhans, and Peter LaFisca. Through the efforts of Col. Joan M. Graziano, a strong supporter of literacy, and many volunteers through the years, the library is a major resource in the community. (Courtesy of John and Bonnie Zurick Jr.)

The Dunbar Lions Club was organized in February 1947. An active group in the community, it was famous for its minstrel shows in the 1950s. Shown are, from left to right, (first row) Huntley Cross, Harry Lizza, Buddy Bigley, unidentified, and Graydon Whipkey; (second row) Paul Miller, William Watson, Wayne Watson Sr., Eugene Baker, Adolph Tristani, Robert Watson, and Albert Hughes. Former mayor of Dunbar and justice of the peace for 15 years, Cross worked for the Western Maryland Railroad and was secretary of the Brotherhood of Railroad Carmen of America. Born in 1911 at Davis, West Virginia, his family later moved to Dunbar where he married Viola Miller and had two children, Huntley and Elizabeth Ann. He was an elder in the Presbyterian Church, a life member of the Dunbar Volunteer Fire Company, and active with the Dunbar Cub Scout pack prior to his death in 1976.

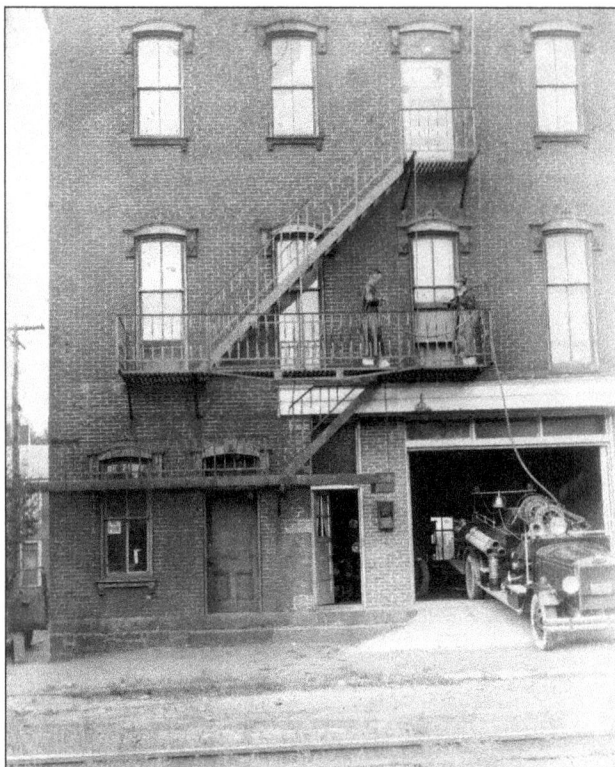

The Dunbar Volunteer Fire Company was organized as the fire brigade in 1916 and chartered in 1923. The first fire truck was purchased in 1928 and housed in Watson's Garage on Woodvale Street. In 1937, the company moved to the Junior's Hall on Railroad Street. This building was owned by Dr. R. W. Clark, who sold it to the Knights of Pythias Lodge No. 410 in 1891. (Courtesy of the Cross family.)

The Dunbar Volunteer Fire Company has a long and proud history in the community, regularly participating in parades and community events. This photograph was taken at the Knights of Pythias building on Railroad Street. Shown in their dress uniforms are, from left to right, Chicken McGivern, Jake Wilhelm, Roy Riser, and Dutch Stroud. (Courtesy of Wayne Watson Jr.)

One of Dunbar's earliest fire trucks was a 1934 Boyer, seen here in front of the Franklin Methodist Church. According to Joseph Trenker, the company raised money to purchase the truck through various fund-raisers including a penny bingo. The money was raised, and the truck was purchased for the whopping sum of $9,900.

Ross May, riding in one of Dunbar's fire trucks, became the Dunbar Volunteer Fire Company's chief shortly after the death of Chief Dutch Stroud in December 1946. In 1951, the company moved from Railroad Street to Connellsville Street where it remained until 1981. In May 1981, the company moved to a new fire station at 1 Fireman's Lane, built at a cost of $83,000. (Courtesy of George R. and Donna R. Myers.)

The Dunbar Volunteer Fire Company has long been involved in water battle competitions. It has many championship trophies that attest to the firefighters' skill in winning the various events in the competition. Shown above are the 1948 firemen receiving the championship trophy. From left to right are Joseph Trenker, Dave Hair, Wayne Watson Jr., Tom Jones, and unidentified. (Courtesy of Wayne Watson Jr.)

The 1940 Scout officials are, from left to right, Joseph Sehee (assistant scoutmaster), Pete Provance (Dunbar Troop 1 scoutmaster), Frank Moore (assistant Dunbar Troop 1 scoutmaster), and Harry Ainsley (Dunbar Troop 1 committee chairman). Sehee, Provance, and Moore were World War II veterans, and Ainsley was a World War I veteran. Seen in the background is Dunbar Motors, owned by Jack Maloy. (Courtesy of Boy Scouts of America Troop 1-180 Archives.)

Wallace Smiley, who became a Scout in 1943, is shown standing on Speers Hill overlooking Dunbar. Visible in the background are, from left to right, (front) the former Dunbar Post Office, now the Dunbar Historical Society; H. P. Smith Meat Market; and the Pennsylvania Railroad station; (back) the George H. Swearingen building and the Presbyterian church. (Courtesy of Wallace Smiley.)

Scouts and leaders prepare to leave on a Canadian trip in 1954. From left to right are (first row) Joseph W. Martin, William Coffman, Ronald Breakiron, Kenneth Martin, and Ronald Leapline; (second row) James I. Bryner (advisor), Fred Bryner, Ray Martin, Samuel Coffman, William F. Rockwell (explorer advisor), and unidentified. Scouting has had a long history in Dunbar and has produced 37 Eagle Scouts over an 80-year period. (Courtesy of Boy Scouts of America Troop 1-180 Archives.)

Dunbar's new Cub Scout Pack 182 charter presentation was held in 1951. First sponsored by the Dunbar Lions Club, it was later sponsored by St. Aloysius Church when the pack number was changed to 180. Today it is sponsored by the Burhans-Crouse Funeral Home. Presenting the charter are, from left to right, (back, center) Edward Hampton, John Graziano, Huntley Cross, and Max Martin (first cub master.) (Courtesy of Jon Marietta.)

Eight
PASTIMES AND COMMUNITY PRIDE

Dunbar was incorporated in 1883, and its centennial celebration was held on June 22–26, 1983. The banner hanging from the balcony of the Hotel Central shows Dunbar's nickname. Since the time of settlers, Dunbar folks have always known how to enjoy themselves. Whatever the occasion, there was a parade. Pastimes have included baseball, football, softball, music, fishing, hunting, scouting, school activities, and community celebrations. Dunbar knows how to celebrate. (Courtesy of Gary Rockwell.)

Held on October 6–9, 1915, Dunbar's old home week was one of the biggest celebrations ever held in town. Every car in the parade had patriotic flags and banners. The town had never seen such elaborate decorations as what graced the buildings, especially the First National Bank and the Hotel Central, where flags and banners hung from every window. The Hotel Central had one of the largest American flags ever displayed in Dunbar. It covered the entire side of the building. A souvenir program was produced for the event that included the historical events of the past century along with a section on Dunbar's industries. The three-day event included races, baseball games, and speeches by James R. Cray on the history of Dunbar and Sen. William E. Crowe, who addressed the huge crowds that were on hand for the event.

Families proudly shared the spotlight with their homes as photographers captured the spirit of the day during the old home week celebration. After three days, the old home week celebration came to an end with the crowning of Dunbar's most popular young lady and its homeliest man. Locally made fireworks were displayed on each day of the event. The people pictured here are unidentified. (Courtesy of Gary Rockwell.)

In the center of town is the new clock dedicated during the 125th anniversary celebration held in June 2008. The theme for the celebration was "Dunbar Our Town," seen on the face of the clock and on T-shirts proudly worn by the people that day. Councilman William Watson and members of the committee suggested the clock to commemorate this milestone in Dunbar's history. (Courtesy of John and Bonnie Zurick Jr.)

LAZY HOUR RANCH, DUNBAR, PA.

One of the East Coast's playgrounds for the rich was Dunbar's Lazy Hour Ranch. A major stop on the East Coast horse show circuit, people came for a week to attend the horse shows, foxhunts, and parties. The ranch was the headquarters of the Chestnut Ridge Hunt Club. There were many jobs for locals who worked in the kitchen while the young men and boys "laid drag" for the hunts and took care of the horses. Trail rides with treks through town to the Dunbar Mountains were common sights. The ranch was used by the U.S. Cavalry to breed and break horses prior to shipping them off to other locations. Mint Alley was a famous army-owned stallion used for breeding purposes whose colts remained at the ranch until they were two years old. (Courtesy of George R. and Donna R. Myers.)

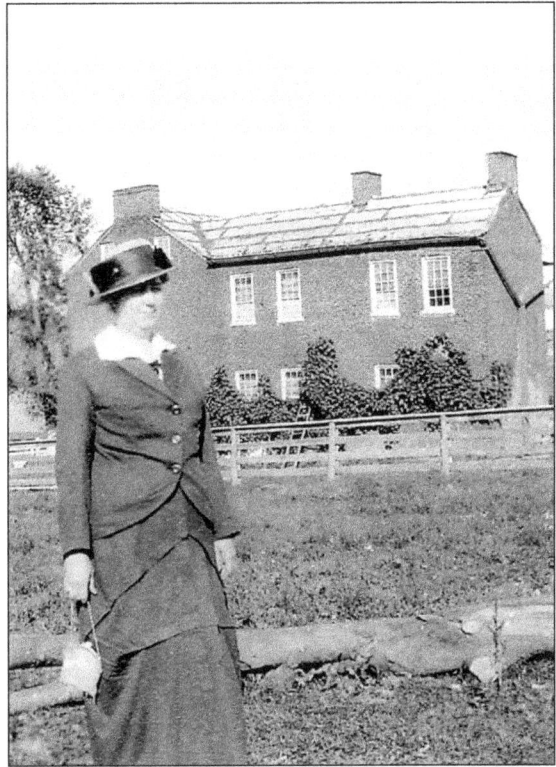

Originally called Deer Park, the Lazy Hour Ranch property was first owned by Capt. George Paull, his son Col. James Paull, and their descendants. It was the third land grant awarded west of the Allegheny Mountains by the crown of England for the Paull family's service during Colonial times. The ranch passed from the Paull family to Henry Cence in 1910. He lost his life when gored by a bull in the barnyard. His son Bertram Cence became owner in 1930 and turned it into the successful Lazy Hour Ranch. The ranch house is shown in the pictures; the woman is unidentified. In 1955, Robert Hall purchased the property in hopes of making it a riding academy and resort. Plans did not work out, the property changed hands again, and it burned down in the early 1960s. (Courtesy of Patricia Paull Newsom.)

Standing majestically at Ye Olde Inn on Route 119 is the stone Native American chief. The chief originally stood at High House near Smithfield in 1951 and was moved to its present location in 1959. Weighing two tons, it is made of local sandstone, with the hands and head made of cement. William (Bill) Warnick, a coal miner and self-taught artist, was born in Dunbar in June 1889. While the stone Native American chief is the most famous of Warnick's works, he created stone carvings at various locations in the Dunbar area. Many believe that the Indian head penny is one of his most intricate stone works. Also an artist, several of his paintings were sold at auction in the 1980s. Warnick died in April 1982 at the age of 92, never having been recognized for his artistic skills. (Courtesy of John and Bonnie Zurick Jr.)

James Bryner is shown standing next to an old millstone near the remains of the Center Furnace. The picture brings credence to the phrase "his stomping grounds were the Dunbar Mountains." A well-respected local, Bryner may be best known for his love of mountain music. From a family that came to this area in the 1700s, he was an old-time fiddler, who only came to playing after the death of his brother "Sheepy" around 1960. Once he tasted the joy of fiddling, he could not put the fiddle down. His repertoire consisted mainly of the songs he grew up with, known as "old southwestern Pennsylvania music." As the superintendent of the Dunbar Sand Corporation, his poem "Ode to Dunbar Sand" showed the depth of sorrow he felt at the sand plant's closing.

Benny Sferro, shown here in 1938, was born in Dunbar in April 1917 and served his country in the army between 1941 and 1945. He loved singing and playing the guitar and became a popular country singer along with his Blue Ridge Mountaineers. His stage name was Benny Dunbar in honor of his hometown, and he sang on WWVA, the Wheeling Jamboree, and WMMN in Fairmont, West Virginia. (Courtesy of Francis Sferro.)

Professionally known as Joe Long, Samuel J. Galterio was a well-known country western singer from the Dunbar area. Along with his band, the Dunbar Mountain Boys, Long played numerous venues around Fayette County during the 1960s and early 1970s. No information is known of the band's disbandment. (Courtesy of Carmella Hardy.)

The lobby card is from the Strand Theatre, one of Dunbar's most popular fun spots. The theater was originally owned and operated by the Rossame family until 1922 when Anthony DeMichelis purchased it. He ran the show until 1961 when Vincent DeMichelis took over. The Strand Theatre closed its doors in 1968, and the building was used for storage and is now a part of the Burhans-Crouse Funeral Home. Kneeling in front of the theater below are Joseph Speeney (left) and James Maddas. First-run movies were shown at the theater during its heyday. During the last years of operation, many youngsters remember the scary B movies shown there and how quickly they ran home after the show to avoid seeing any of the sinister creatures from the movies.

The Most Eagerly-Awaited Motion Picture of All Time

GONE WITH THE WIND

Among the Players

Rhett Butler
  CLARK GABLE
Scarlett O'Hara
  VIVIEN LEIGH
Ashley Wilkes
  LESLIE HOWARD
Melanie Hamilton
  OLIVIA de HAVILLAND
Gerald O'Hara
  THOMAS MITCHELL
Mammy *HATTIE McDANIEL*
Ellen O'Hara
  BARBARA O'NEIL
Belle Watling *ONA MUNSON*
Aunt "Pittypat" Hamilton
  LAURA HOPE CREWS
Frank Kennedy *CARROLL NYE*
Doctor Meade
  HARRY DAVENPORT
India Wilkes *ALICIA RHETT*
Charles Hamilton
  RAND BROOKS
Suellen O'Hara
  EVELYN KEYES
Carreen O'Hara
  ANN RUTHERFORD
Prissy *BUTTERFLY McQUEEN*
Pork *OSCAR POLK*
Jonas Wilkerson *VICTOR JORY*
Uncle Peter
  EDDIE ANDERSON
Stuart Tarleton *FRED CRANE*
Brent Tarleton
  GEORGE REEVES
Mrs. Merriwether
  JANE DARWELL
Sam *EVERETT BROWN*
thousands more!

FULL LENGTH! NOTHING CUT BUT THE PRICE!

STRAND
THEATRE   Dunbar, Pa.

WEDNESDAY AND THURSDAY
APRIL 16 - 17

DAVID O. SELZNICK'S production of
MARGARET MITCHELL'S
Story of the Old South
GONE WITH THE WIND
IN TECHNICOLOR starring
Clark GABLE as Rhett Butler
Leslie
HOWARD • DeHAVILLAND
and genuine
Vivien LEIGH as Scarlett O'Hara
A Selznick International Production

Starts at 3:30 P. M. - 2 Shows Daily

ADMISSION - UP TO 5 P. M.
Adults 25c Children 40c 25c

AFTER 5 P. M.
All Admission 55c, Federal Tax Included

NOTE - All Children Must Pay

John Picus (Jack) Quinn was born Johannes (Jan) Pajkos (1883–1946) in Slovakia and immigrated to America with his parents in 1884. He came to Dunbar in 1901 where he worked for the Dunbar Furnace and played recreational ball for mining teams. While watching a game in Connellsville, he threw an errant pitch from the stands back to the catcher. A manager from Dunbar was impressed by the throw and offered him a contract. He started pitching for the local team. In 1906, he was playing semiprofessional ball. After a few years in the minor leagues, he made his major-league debut with the New York Highlanders (Yankees) in 1909. Pitching for 23 years, he started in 443 games, winning 247 for eight different teams. He played until he was 50 years old, with his final game on July 7, 1933. He died at age 62 in Pottsville. (Courtesy of Patrick Maloy.)

Dunbar won the WPA-YMCA Junior Baseball League, defeating Connellsville Hilltop in a best-of-three series. Jim Jarvis won the first game pitching a 10-0 shutout. Cutty Caruso turned in a masterful performance of relief pitching and received credit for the win in the final game. Pictured are, from left to right, (first row) batboy E. K. Strong; (second row) Donald DeBerry, Allen Hamilton, Cutty Caruso, Bob Dunaway, Jim Jarvis, Fred Lizza, Gerald Rossi, and John Bruno; (third row) Fran Miskinnis, Eddie Mahan, Felix Manzola, Francis Schwenning, Willie Lizza, Marcus DeMarco, Red McDowell, Wayne Hamilton, and Rev. W. S. Hamilton. Below is one of Dunbar's baseball teams from the 1920s. From left to right are (first row) Jim Gilmore, Ronald Cross, Jack Maloy, Clarence "Dash" Harvey, Ray Trimbath, Lawrence Grass, and Greek Bruno; (second row) George Trimbath, Todd Burhans, Frank George, Harvey Ainsley, Albert Harvey, Gordon Topper, and Frank Grass.

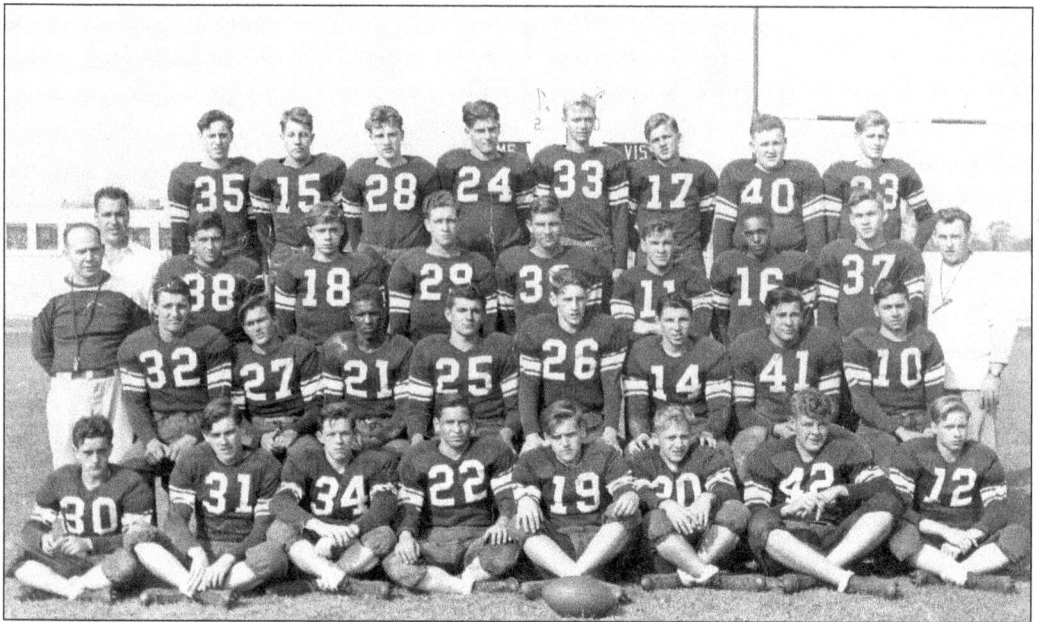

The 1946 Dunbar Township Mules football team was one of the many tough, hard-nosed teams in Fayette County. The team, named after the mules used to haul coal out of the many mines located in and around Dunbar, had three players from town known as the "Green Mountain Boys." Among those pictured are (third row, center) Arnold Brubaker (29), Donald Hardy (39), and Dearl Lowry (11).

Crowned 1947 Fayette County champions, this Dunbar team defeated Leckrone in the best-of-five series. Pictured are, from left to right, (first row) John Variano, Joseph "Red" Bowman, Anthony Viher, John Bruno, Mike Kremposky, Henry Smith (scorekeeper), Bob Martinchalk, and Bud Bigley; (second row) Arnold Brubaker, Herb Humphrey (business manager), Stan McLaughlin, Clarence "Dash" Harvey, Tom Lyons, Mike Krall, Joe Krall, Jack Maloy (manager), Joseph "Brud" Courtney, John Bugosky, and Hugh Dunaway (coach).

These three dams on Dunbar Creek were originally built for use by the Pennsylvania Wire Glass Company and the Dunbar Sand Corporation's downstream operations, which are now closed. Dunbar Creek is one of the finest trout streams in the country. From its mountain headwaters to its flow through Dunbar to the Youghiogheny River, the stream is an important part of the landscape. Thanks to work by volunteer groups like the Dunbar Sportsmen Club, the stream is now as pristine as it was before any industry intruded upon it. The importance of the creek cannot be understated. The Dunbar Sportsmen Club, organized in 1952 and chartered in 1954, has a proud history of promoting conservation, fishing, and hunting in the Dunbar area and regularly sponsors youth programs on a variety of sporting topics. (Courtesy of Mary D. Ryan.)

Some of Dunbar's residents took vacations to places near and far. Here H. P. Smith (back, right) and his wife, Annie McPherson Smith (front, right), along with an unidentified couple on the left, show off the swimsuits of the day as they pose for this beach picture. H. P. Smith owned a meat market in Dunbar and was a well-respected citizen of the town. (Courtesy of Warren Wortman.)

Nine

DUNBAR TODAY

Formed in 1995, the Dunbar Historical Society met in the Dunbar Library and local churches. The society purchased a small park area in the middle of town in 2005 and in 2006 purchased the former post office building across the street from the park. The major goal of the society is to preserve Dunbar's history so future generations can learn about their heritage.

FUTURE SITE OF A BEEHIVE OVEN

DUNBAR HISTORICAL SOCIETY

While the industrial base is gone, Dunbar is poised to take advantage of several tourism opportunities that will help revitalize the town. The Dunbar Historical Society is rebuilding a coke oven at its park across the street from the education center. In 2006, the Fayette Central Railroad tourist train began runs between Dunbar and Uniontown. Since that time, almost 10,000 people have taken the train ride. In 2008, the Sheepskin Trail, the first spur off the Great Allegheny Passage, was opened to bikers and walkers. Exercise equipment was placed along the trail and, thanks to the work of former councilwoman Kathleen Dynes, a new playground area was open for the town's children. Dunbar is fortunate to have Dunbar Creek flowing through the middle of town. It is considered one of the country's top trout-fishing streams, and anglers come from far and wide to fish there. As the "gateway to the beautiful Dunbar Mountains," Dunbar's tourism future looks bright.

A celebration was held on August 24, 2006, when the Dunbar Historical Society purchased the historic post office, which was built around 1900. A ribbon-cutting ceremony was held. From left to right are Michael J. Bell (treasurer), George R. Myers (president), John Zurick Jr. (vice president), Col. Joan M. Graziano (founding member), Angela Zimmerlink (Fayette County commissioner), and life members Pat Caruso, Oliver Wayne Martin, and Robert M. Martin.

The park photograph shows the area where the coke oven will be built. The cut stones at left will be used in the park design. In 2008, unused coke oven materials were located and moved to the site in preparation for building the coke oven. The millstone was donated by Phyllis and Arnold Brubaker, Cindy Moag, and Lois Moag, and installed by Frank Wallace.

The Fayette Central Railroad Richmond, Fredericksburg and Potomac Railroad Alco S2 engine (left) is decorated for its inaugural run on Memorial Day in 2006. Built in 1948, it pulled a Pittsburg and Lake Erie Railroad bay window caboose and a Penn Central Railroad transfer caboose. The Fayette Central Railroad also runs a Budd RDC-1 Balitmore and Ohio Railroad 9913 car (below) leased from the Baltimore and Ohio Railroad Museum. In the 1890s, the Baltimore and Ohio Railroad acquired the Fairmont, Morgantown and Pittsburgh Railroad and 11 miles of track from Uniontown to the Baltimore and Ohio main line. Regular passenger service ended in 1953. In the 1980s, the Chessie System removed the tracks from Smithfield, Pennsylvania, to Morgantown, West Virginia, and in 1996 sold the remaining line to the Fay-Penn Industrial Development Corporation. For more information, visit the Fayette Central Railroad Web site. (Left, courtesy of George R. and Donna R. Myers; below, courtesy of Dave Moffett.)

The Sheepskin Trail officially opened on May 29, 2008. The 2.1-mile trail connects to the Youghiogheny River Trail, part of the Great Allegheny Passage at Wheeler near Connellsville (above), and enters Dunbar Borough next to the Dunbar Historical Society (below). The Sheepskin Trail is the first leg of the 32-mile-long trail that will cut through the center of Fayette County and continue on to Point Marion. It will connect to the West Virginia Rail-Trail System at the state line and will connect to the American Discovery Trail. This is a 6,300-mile-long trail system that goes from Cape Henlopen State Park in Delaware to Point Reyes National Seashore in California.

Started in 2002, the Dunbar Community Fest is held each year on the last Saturday of September. First sponsored by the Dunbar Historical Society, the success of the festival has allowed it to become a separate organization. With a parade (above), car show, daylong entertainment, poker run, Pechin five-kilometer race and walk, flea market, train rides, duck race, kids' games, historical displays, quilt show, and food galore, it is a homecoming day for many former residents. Taking part in the parade in a fire truck (below) once owned by his grandfather Pechin founder Sullivan D'Amico are Donald D'Amico Jr. and his wife, Krista D'Amico, and child Carson D'Amico. (Above, courtesy of Michael J. Bell; below, courtesy of Krista D'Amico.)

BIBLIOGRAPHY

Bayard, Samuel. *Hill Country Tunes: Instrumental Folk Music of Southwestern Pennsylvania.* Philadelphia: American Folklore Society, 1944.

Crowe, William. *History of Dunbar, Pennsylvania and Vicinity.* Dunbar, PA: Self-published, 1939.

Family Member. *Family Historical Register of (Van) Swearingen Family.* Washington, D.C.: C. W. Brown, 1884.

Gresham, John M., and Samuel T. Wiley. *Biographical and Portrait Cyclopedia of Fayette County, Pennsylvania.* Chicago: Gresham and Company, 1889.

Hickok, W. O., and F. T. Moyer. *Geology and Mineral Resources of Fayette County, Pennsylvania.* Harrisburg, PA: Pennsylvania Department of Internal Affairs, 1940.

Miner, Mark A. "Aled-Ha. Fayette County's Forgotten Mountain Poet." *Western Pennsylvania History* 82, No. 3 (fall 1999).

Morrison, Donald, and the Centennial Committee. *Dunbar: The Furnace Town.* Dunbar, PA: Self-published, 1983.

Myers, Donna. *Celebrating 125 Years: Dunbar, Pennsylvania 1884–2008.* Dunbar, PA: Dunbar Historical Society, 2008.

Myers, Donna, and Bonnie Zurick. *There's No Place Like Dunbar.* Bookman Publishing, 2005.

Nelson, S. B. *Nelson's Biographical Dictionary and Historical Reference Book of Fayette County, Pennsylvania.* Uniontown, PA: Nelson Publisher, 1900.

Powell, Allan. *Christopher Gist, Frontier Scout.* Shippensburg, PA: Burd Street Press, 1992.

Ray, William Stanley. *Annual Report of the Pennsylvania State College for the Year 1897.* State Printer of Pennsylvania, 1898.

Sipe, C. Hale. *The Indian Wars of Pennsylvania.* Harrisburg, PA: Telegraph Press, 1929.

Stewart, Thomas J. *Pennsylvania Department of Internal Affairs Part V: Reports of Inspectors of Coal Mines.* State Printer of Pennsylvania, 1890.

Young, William. "New Haven and Dunbar, Pennsylvania." *Seven Short-Lines, Their Lives and Times.* Susquehanna, PA: Starrucca Valley Publishing, 1961.

Visit us at
arcadiapublishing.com

....